Asi

ASIA
MELTDOWN

THE END
OF THE
MIRACLE?

Leo Gough

CAPSTONE

First Published 1998
Capstone Publishing Limited
Oxford Centre for Innovation
Mill Street
Oxford OX2 0JX
United Kingdom
http://www.capstone.co.uk

British Library Cataloguing in Publication Data
A CIP catalogue record for this book is available from the British Library

ISBN 1-900961-91-1

Typeset in 10/14 Zapf Calligraphic by
Sparks Computer Solutions, Oxford
http://www.sparks.co.uk
Printed and bound by
T.J. International Ltd, Padstow, Cornwall

This book is printed on acid-free paper

To Claudia

Contents

Acknowledgements

I would like to thank Professor Jae Ho Park, Romesh Vaitlingam, Jet Magsaysay of *World Executive Digest*, the Centre for Economic Policy Research (UK), Dean LeBaron, and others who asked not to be named for the generous help they gave me during the writing of this book. Needless to say, any errors of fact and, unless otherwise indicated, opinions are the sole responsibility of the author. I'd also like to thank the publishers, Richard Burton and Mark Allin, for their hearty support, Tom Fryer of Sparks for getting the book to the printer in record time, and Kim Tompkins and Mandie Bradshaw of FT Profile for their kind assistance.

Capstone would like to acknowledge the enormous contribution of Barney Allan of Anorak and Ian Pringle of APD Singapore.

The Way We Were

It was a hot evening in July. Jimmy Siang relaxed as he sipped his drink in the clubhouse overlooking the golf course he'd partly financed and contemplated his affairs. Life was good. His two grown-up daughters were married and living in the USA and his son was in his third year at university in Sydney. No worries there, though it hadn't been easy at times to pay for their foreign education.

He thought about his businesses; these days he had his fingers in quite a few pies – a piece of a logging company in neighbouring Indonesia, rental properties in London and Vancouver, and shares in several real estate projects in his native Kuala Lumpur. But these were all passive investments – he didn't have time to run them personally. His real pride and joy would always be the advertising agency he'd inherited from his father which he'd managed ever since the old man died 20 years ago.

Jimmy had seen his agency grow rapidly; he now employed more than 40 people full time and his clients were prestigious – big name Korean and Japanese manufacturers, for the most part, eager to introduce new products to the mass markets of Malaysia and next-door Indonesia.

Most of his employees were Chinese and Indian. Like his competitors, his biggest problem was always in finding enough qualified staff to keep up with the pace of change and the strident demands of his overseas clients, but as he mentally reviewed his employees, he felt reasonably comfortable. Unlike his tyrannical father, Jimmy liked to give younger talent its head, and he was very pleased with his executives, all in their twenties and educated abroad – they were real pros. He also was well satisfied with the rather dangerous experiment of employing some Euro-

pean creative talent; they'd settled down nicely, and had enabled the agency to swing some very large accounts which otherwise would have gone elsewhere. At least he could fire them if things went wrong – unlike his local staff, who were heavily protected by the country's employment laws.

A friend sat down in the chair beside him and started to boast about his stock market winnings. Jimmy humoured the man politely; as far as he was personally concerned the stock market was a mystery which he had neither the time nor the inclination to fathom. Unlike many of his countrymen, Jimmy was no gambler and he didn't believe that they knew what they were doing with their share investments. His business friends often teased him about this 'old-fashioned' attitude, but he was unconcerned – conversations with Kwai Lo ('white ghosts', a Chinese term for Caucasians) had convinced him that the average Kwai Lo professional didn't know anything about the stock market either.

Next morning at the office, Jimmy's chief account executive was waiting to see him. A Japanese client was preparing a massive campaign which would mean several hundred thousand dollars' worth of profit for the agency before the end of the year. They discussed their plans briefly. As he left, the executive remarked, 'Did you see the news? The Thais have devalued the baht.' Jimmy shrugged – he had no business in Thailand.

That was when the hell started. All through July and August the Malaysian ringgit dropped, massively increasing the overheads of the agency and the cost of the money Jimmy sent abroad to his son. Thailand and Indonesia were in chaos, and it was affecting his business after all – advertising budgets seemed to be heading downwards fast.

Jimmy was used to nasty surprises; his response was to pressurise his executives to look for business wherever they could get it. The big accounts would never dry up completely, he thought, but he wanted to see the company cover its overheads every month without fail – there was no way he was going to put any more capital into the business.

Then in September the haze came – a choking yellow chemical-tasting smog hanging over a vast area of Indonesia and Malaysia. Light planes were crashing in

Borneo, where the haze was thickest. No-one seemed to know what had caused it at first, but it was no great surprise when it was finally admitted in late September that forest fires were raging across Indonesia, evidently started by companies, both local and foreign, who were eager to clear land before stricter environmental laws were introduced.

The haze wasn't too bad around Jimmy's house up on a hill in Kuala Lumpur's smartest residential district. You couldn't see much from the windows, but at least you could breathe. Downtown, you could barely see in front of your face at times and people were getting badly sick. Jimmy's wife wanted to go to Thailand until the haze cleared up – all the wives wanted to go, as a group. 'Fine', said Jimmy, 'Just don't spend too much money. What happens if the haze never clears up?'

By October the haze was beginning to clear, and there was less of a sense of apocalypse in South East Asia. Now everyone was talking about the IMF bailouts of Thailand and Indonesia, and whether it would happen in Malaysia. Jimmy wasn't interested in macroeconomic waffle, but it was plain that there was no more boom; the government was postponing its big projects and the ringgit just kept on going down. Jimmy's own real estate projects were stalled. Property prices and rents in Kuala Lumpur seemed to be dropping.

The next month brought really bad news. South Korea was virtually bankrupt. All those massive Korean accounts virtually dried up overnight – the Koreans seemed to be in a total state of shock. The company was barely profitable, but local clients were desperately seeking new business, so they were still advertising. Jimmy called a halt to all the company's expansion plans and increased the pressure on his executives to bring in business, even low prestige stuff, just to pay the bills.

The turn of the year brought Malaysia's endless series of holidays, so it wasn't until the spring that the action started again. Things weren't looking quite so bad. The company had retrenched adequately for the time being and was ticking over.

Jimmy's a survivor. He's seen too many booms and busts in his lifetime to believe in miracles; for him, business is always about the long term and the bottom line. I think he's going to make it.

This book is about the financial crisis in Asia. To understand what has happened and its implications, we need to look at the affected countries as they were during the extraordinary spurt of growth which began in the late 1980s. Each country is different, but all of them, despite their success in modernisation, are volatile by the standards of the West. The seeds of a bust always exist in a boom. As we will see, the perennial difficulty is to judge the difference between 'genuine' growth and mere extravagance. Like other countries, the Asian nations are capable of both. It remains to be seen how the crisis will be resolved, so this book can only give an interim picture – no-one knows how the events of 1997 will appear in the hindsight of five years' time.

Since the middle of the 1980s the world has been listening to tales of the apparently miraculous success of the developing economies of Asia. Singapore and Hong Kong were well-known as tiny city states that were expanding their financial services, but more attention was paid to those Asian countries, such as South Korea, Malaysia, and Indonesia, which were playing increasingly dramatic manufacturing roles. By 1993 Japan began to relocate its factories in other Asian countries, as had Korea and Taiwan, to take advantage of lower labour costs. China is as yet too undeveloped to benefit from these moves, which have mainly been to South East Asian nations.

Commodity exporters like Brunei, Malaysia and Indonesia had, before the late 1980s, concentrated on building their manufacturing capacity while protecting it from foreign competition. Trade liberalisation only began in the late 1980s as money poured in from Japan, Korea and Taiwan.

With rapid growth comes debt. In the mid-1980s there had been a number of financial crises in South East Asia. In Thailand in 1984, for example, too much credit caused a devaluation of the baht. Indonesia suffered two devaluations, a property crash and reduced foreign investment when oil prices dropped. Malaysia had to reduce its industrialisation plans in 1985 when foreign financiers lost confidence in the country's ability to service its debt. The Philippines, still suffering under Marcos, was in desperate financial trouble. Vietnam devalued twice and suffered huge unemployment between 1984 and 1988.

As the region recovered, efforts were made to liberalise the financial markets, partly in response to foreign investors' demands for such facilities as currency hedges for exports, partly due to pressure from international financial institutions who wished to establish themselves more fully and partly because a global free market is the stated policy aim of the economic giants, the US and Japan. South East Asia was willing both to allow non-residents to move money in and out of their countries freely and to purchase property – freeing capital movement – and also to free the financial markets to allow investment by locals and foreigners in foreign currency deposits, domestic bonds, and the local stock markets.

This kind of liberalisation has been extremely attractive to foreign investors who seek liquidity and good short-term returns – hence the 'Asian miracle' – but it is also a major factor in the current crisis. Yet every country in the region is unique, so to understand the events of 1997 we should look at each of the principal nation-players in the economic drama as they were at the beginning of that year.

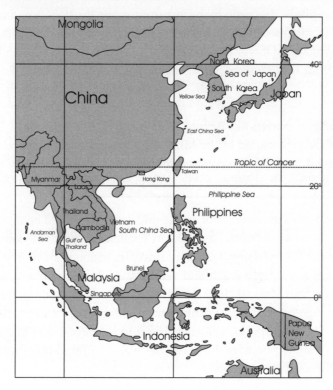

The Newly Industrialised Countries: Malaysia, Indonesia, the Philippines and Thailand

Malaysia

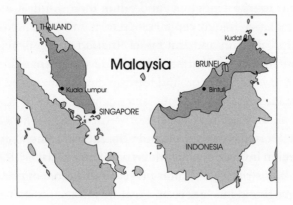

Malaysia borders Thailand in the Malay Peninsula and Indonesia on the large island of Borneo. It is populated by three main groups – the indigenous Malay groups (47%), Chinese, who dominate business life (32%) and Indians (8%). Colonised by the British, Malaysia became fully independent in 1963. In 1965 Singapore seceded from the Federation and became an independent republic. Its political system is based upon the British parliamentary model. With a relatively small population (approximately 20 million) and very high literacy, the country was enjoying GDP growth of over 8% until the currency crisis. Its major markets are Singapore (20%), the US (18%), the EU (14%) and Japan (13%).

Malaysia has rich natural resources, is a leading exporter of tin, rubber, palm oil and tropical hardwoods and has large reserves of petroleum and natural gas. The country is the world's top producer of natural rubber. Growth in the last few years has concentrated on a switch from agriculture to manufacturing. In 1996, GDP contribution from manufacturing was 34.3%, wholesale, retail trade and hotels, government services, finance, insurance and real estate was 31.1%, agriculture, forestry and fishing was 12.4%, mining was 7% and construction was 4.4%.

One of the main issues facing the Malaysian Government is how to improve the economic power of the Malay majority while maintaining racial harmony with the economically dominant Chinese minority. A policy favouring bumiputra (Malay) owned enterprises has been in place for many years.

As a member of the six-nation Association of South East Asian Nations (ASEAN), Malaysia is involved in the establishment of a 'growth triangle' project with Thailand and Indonesia. Infrastructure development has grown dramatically, concentrating on the development of highways, water and forestry projects, port and tourism development and the building of industrial parks.

Freedom from exchange controls and a liberalised economy has brought a flood of foreign investment into Malaysia, along with its 13 free zones. Ten FIZs (Free Industrial Zones) offer investors duty-free importation of raw materials, parts and machinery and feature minimal customs control and formalities. One FCZ (Free Commercial Zone) is designed for establishments engaged in training, breaking bulk, grading, repacking, relabelling and transit. The other two free zones are for trading in export products. The government has instituted a large number of attractive incentives for foreign manufacturers and high-tech workers.

Malaysia is a constitutional monarchy, nominally headed by the Yang di-Pertuan Agong, customarily referred to as the King, who is elected for a five-year term from the nine sultans of the peninsular Malaysian states. True executive power is held by the cabinet, led by the charismatic prime minister Datuk Seri Dr Mahathir bin Mohamad who has presided, since 1981, over Malaysia's transformation from a tin and rubber producer at the end of World War II to a widely diversified economy. The 1981–82 world recession depressed the country's commodity exports and led to a serious increase in debt, from $4 billion in 1980 to $15 billion in 1984. In 1985 Malaysia plunged into a serious recession but was recovering by 1987. For the next three years, GDP growth was over 10% annually, resulting from a successful drive to increase exports of manufactured goods. Since then growth has dropped a little, to around 8%, but there has been significant expansion of production in industries producing electrical and electronic products, chemicals and chemical products, non-metallic mineral products and transport equipment. Construction has boomed, and by the beginning of 1997 there were clear signs of oversupply.

Indonesia

The largest archipelago in the world, Indonesia is a unique and beautiful, yet undeveloped, country. Its success in economic growth is all the more remarkable given its situation – it has more than 17,000 islands of which only 6000 are settled – and a vast population of 200 million. A multiracial, multilingual society, Indonesia has political difficulties which will not go away. The government, dominated by President Soeharto, has operated a succession of five-year plans since the 1970s to develop the economy. In the early 1990s industrial growth was over 9% a year and the contribution of the sector to the country's GDP surged from 9.2% in 1969 to 22.3% in 1993.

Indonesia has a free-market economy but the government still plays a significant role through state-owned firms and the imposition of price controls in selected industries. Since President Soeharto took power in 1966, Indonesia's economy has grown steadily, from a per capita GNP of $70 to a per capita GNP of about $900. Real GDP growth has been more than 6% annually during the 1990s while inflation has stayed low and the country has enjoyed trade surpluses.

The main export is petroleum and the country suffers when world oil prices fall. In the mid-1980s, the government began to liberalise the economy. Import obstacles are still up, however.

The oil and gas sector, including refining, is about 10% of GDP. As domestic demand increases, Indonesia is expected to become a net importer of oil by the next century. The state owns all oil and mineral rights and foreign contractors operate through partnerships.

Known as an important source of bauxite, silver, and tin production, Indonesia is expanding its copper, nickel, gold, and coal output for export markets. Total coal production reached 41 million tonnes in 1996, including exports of 27 million tonnes.

Japan is the biggest foreign investor in Indonesia, followed by Singapore, Hong Kong, Taiwan, and South Korea. Most approved investment during the last few years has been in manufacturing, especially in textile, pulp and paper, and chemical industries. The investment climate has improved with privatisation moves.

Heavy industry is oriented towards the domestic market and designed to help stimulate internal growth. Consumer electronics are growing rapidly but there are few exports. Car production is growing annually by over 20%.

Basic chemical manufacturing, such as agro-chemicals to improve food production, rubber processing and paper manufacturing, have all grown rapidly.

In 1950 Indonesia became independent from the Dutch. At the time of independence, the Dutch retained control over the western half of New Guinea, known as Irian Jaya. After negotiations failed armed clashes broke out in the area between Indonesian and Dutch troops in 1961. In 1962 Indonesia took over sovereignty of Irian Jaya. In 1976, the country annexed East Timor, a Portuguese colony on the island of Timor. Timor and Irian Jaya remain to this day sources of political unrest; however there have been a succession of rebellions and massacres throughout the archipelago. General Soeharto took over from General Sukarno in 1966 and re-established economic development as the government's main goal.

Although nominally independent, the judiciary is strongly influenced by the government, and military officers serve in the civilian bureaucracy at all government levels. While the country remains, in Western eyes, under an autocratic regime, further economic development is seen as the key to reducing tensions.

Indonesia is one of the highest performing Asian economies, although it is starting from a low base. GDP growth per person and figures for the reduction of poverty are impressive. The World Bank judged that Indonesia moved from low to lower middle-income country status in 1993.

Philippines

Once known as the 'Sick Man of Asia', this former US colony has for the first time been showing some positive economic signs during the last few years. Hitherto, mismanagement and gross human exploitation had been the rule, not least under the Marcos regime – the country of 7000 islands, which is rich in resources and agriculture, had an annual per capita GDP growth rate of only 1.6% between 1965 and 1989.

When Marcos fell and Corey Aquino became leader in 1986, things began to improve. The US and Japan began to pump millions into the economy.

Promised reforms, however, did not take place. When President Ramos came to power in 1992, the problem of poverty was seriously addressed for the first time. Recent data suggests that the poverty level is decreasing (from 50% in 1961 to 36% in 1994). In 1996 Ramos managed to remove 60% of the population from their liability to income tax.

The Ramos government successfully initiated a privatisation programme of the nation's telecommunications, telephone systems, utilities, transportation, and shipping ports. In 1992, the government invested $1 billion in modernising the electrical power sector. By 1994 this had resulted in an 18% increase in electrical supply. These improvements to the infrastructure enabled Filipino companies to borrow far more abroad and began to attract capital back into the country. In 1994 and 1995 the government was able to report a budget surplus – truly a miracle, in the eyes of many observers. The 1995 GNP growth was 5.7%, the highest ever in the nation's history. Since then there has been talk of the Philippines becoming economically independent, perhaps even outstripping Indonesia in development.

In early 1997, *Asia Week* was able to say:

> *'The outlook is bright. Infrastructure, construction and property development should remain strong, and manufacturing is expected to be robust. Deregulation could energize the finance, telecommunications, transportation and insurance industries. Not just that: the retail sector may open to foreigners. Exports are expected to grow as should investment into the nation. 1997 may be remembered as the year the Philippines economy became truly integrated with the rest of the world's. And a traditional strength – money from overseas workers such as maids – could well also help fuel the home economy. A threat: politics could shift attention from economic planning and reform to partisanship as jockeying heats up among potential successors in 1998.'*

In fact, despite the currency crisis, the economy did manage to grow by 5.8% in 1997. The recent liberalisation has resulted in a vibrant telecommunications industry. The market for telecommunications equipment and services is predicted to spurt with the implementing of a national information highway. Electrical power, construction and chemical manufacturing are all well established.

Thailand

Until mid-1997, Thailand was synonymous with the Asian miracle; it had apparently succeeded in developing an open market economy based on a free enterprise system. Despite frequent changes in government, Thai leaders were widely believed to have pursued consistently conservative fiscal and monetary policies. Growth in GDP averaged over 8% for the preceding ten years, and over 10% between 1988 and 1994.

The main growth sectors are:

- Manufacturing – a diversified manufacturing sector makes the largest contribution to the economy. Successful export industries include automatic data processing machines, radios and televisions, rubber, footwear, and integrated circuits.
- Agriculture – although more than half of Thailand's workers are still on the land (the country's population is 59 million) and the sector is still growing, the relative size of agriculture's contribution to GDP continues to decline.
- Construction – 'overheating' occurred in real estate in 1990, and since then doubts have risen as to whether the annual growth of around 8% can be sustained indefinitely.
- Tourism – tourism earns Thailand over $5.5 billion a year but fluctuates according to external events affecting foreign visitors.

Rapid growth has caused severe degradation of the natural environment and Bangkok's infrastructure is straining at the seams. Plans for more power plants, ports, airports, telephone lines, roads, trains, a new administrative city and sewage treatment plants for all major cities are in train.

The Thai government controls a sizeable number of utilities and infrastructure companies, but overall the public sector employs only 4.4% of the workforce. From 1984 the Thai baht was pegged to a basket of currencies of principal trading partners. The composition of the basket is a closely guarded secret, but the US dollar appears to represent well over half of the value of the basket. The Thai baht averaged around 25 to US$1 from 1987 to 1997.

The government has liberalised the foreign exchange system and banks allow private individuals to hold accounts in foreign currencies. Repatriation of investment capital is allowed and reporting requirements have been reduced.

Thailand is a member of the Association of South East Asian Nations (ASEAN). In 1992 ASEAN governments approved a Thai proposal to establish the ASEAN Free Trade Area (AFTA), which is intended to virtually eliminate tariffs on products traded among ASEAN countries by the year 2007. AFTA is a market of over \$400 billion.

The country has a history of frequent changes in government, political violence and military intervention. Economic policies have, however, remained friendly to foreign business throughout all domestic difficulties.

The dragons: Hong Kong, Singapore, South Korea and Taiwan

Hong Kong

Until July 1997 Hong Kong was a British colony. It consists of the Kowloon peninsula, the New Territories, the business and residential area, and Hong Kong island where most of the financial and administrative faculties are concentrated, as well as over 200 tiny islands, mostly uninhabited. The population is 6 million – about double that of Singapore. The vast majority of the population (95%) are Chinese, principally from China's neighbouring Canton province and also from Shanghai. Hong Kong was seized by Britain after the First Opium War (1840–1842) and the land was subsequently formally leased to Britain by China in 1898. By the turn of the century, Hong Kong had become the principal distribution centre for British trade with China. In 1949 many hundreds of thousands of Chinese fled to Hong Kong following the communist victory in mainland China.

In 1996, Hong Kong's GDP was nearly $154 billion, easily outstripping that of, say, Great Britain. Its growth rate has hovered around 6% in recent years. The territory is in the world's top ten list of trading nations and is arguably the richest and most successful of the 'Dragon' economies. It has almost no natural resources and can produce less than 20% of its own food; its principal natural asset is its magnificent harbour.

Hong Kong's main trading partners are China, the United States, Japan, Taiwan, Germany, Singapore, and South Korea. With its modern communications, transportation, and banking facilities, as well as extensive expertise in trade and investment with China, Hong Kong has major importance in world's economy. Growing quickly in the 1980s, there was a setback after the Chinese Tiananmen Square debacle in 1989 but Hong Kong rebounded quickly.

Services now make up about 75% of GDP, having long overtaken manufacturing as the engine of growth – most manufacturing (clothing and toys) is now done in mainland China. The major components of Hong Kong's service sector are shipping, civil aviation, tourism, and financial services. Financial and business services include banking, insurance, real estate and a wide range of other professional services. Like Singapore, Hong Kong's strategic location and its excellent communications network and efficient infrastructure have made it a hub for trade, finance and business services in the region.

Until the Asian currency crisis began in mid-1997, the big story in the region was Hong Kong's handover to China. On 1 July 1997, China took over the sovereignty of Hong Kong. The government of Chief Executive Tung Chee Hwa was installed on that date. The elected Legislative Council was disbanded, but most of the institutions and the vast majority of the senior civil servants who oversee the daily operations of the Hong Kong SAR remained unchanged. The Sino-British Joint Declaration of 1984 provided the framework for this peaceful transfer, stipulating that Hong Kong would become a Special Administrative Region of the People's Republic of China but would retain a high degree of autonomy in all matters except foreign and defence affairs. The Joint Declaration further stated that for 50 years after reversion Hong Kong would retain its political, economic, and judicial systems, and could continue participating in international agreements and organisations under the name, 'Hong Kong, China'.

Hong Kong's real test as a Special Administrative Region of China is only just beginning. While the facade of the colonial government continues, elections will be less open as China does not want dissident politicians to be elected. One danger is that lower-income groups will be ignored in favour of powerful elites though Western pressure should prevent China from behaving too heavy-handedly. In the long term, however, Hong Kong may not retain its economic vitality – the city is already the most expensive in the world, and the government relies heavily on taxes on inflated land transactions. Its future remains uncertain.

Singapore

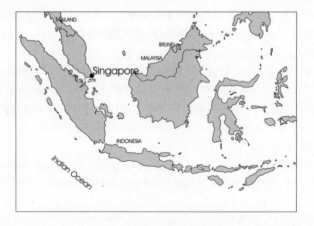

Singapore consists of one main island and 54 small ones at the southern tip of the Malay peninsula. It has a highly educated population of only three million, who are predominantly south Chinese.

Founded in 1819 by Stamford Raffles, Singapore rapidly became an important trading centre in the region. Since independence it has been dominated by the authoritarian, Oxford-educated Lee Quan Yu. From 1963 to 1965 the country was part of Malaysia, but was expelled from the federation when it refused to implement Malaysian laws intended to favour ethnic Malays over ethnic Chinese in business. At the time, Lee Quan Yu was publicly fearful that the city-state would not survive on its own.

By the 1970s, Singapore had become one of the top industrial nations of the region; the trade generated by its port is the world's second largest. Economic growth in recent years has averaged 10% and, like neighbouring countries, it is rapidly developing its information technology and banking sectors. In 1996 the OECD removed Singapore from its 'developing country' list.

Singapore is so small that it must export to survive; thus it grows along with the growth of larger neighbours. Singapore's port acts both as the trading and distribution hub for the economies of South East Asia, as well as the major transhipment point linking the region to the rest of the world. In addition to trade, it also acts as a financial centre for the region as a whole. With the success of the economy, the control of business overheads and the need to stay competitive are major concerns. Singapore has had huge balance of payments and budget surpluses for years.

Inflation has been low – hovering under 3% – and growth began to 'slow' in 1995 to 8%, still remarkable by world standards. The steady appreciation of the Singapore dollar, which has kept the price of imports low, has been Singapore's main tool for controlling inflation, though there are fears it is hurting Singapore's export competitiveness.

Manufacturing makes up 27% and financial/business services 29% of GDP.

Rising demand for private housing caused the construction sector to grow by nearly 16% in 1994. Within manufacturing, electronics is the most important industry: Singapore manufactures roughly half of the world's supply of computer disk drives, and exports significant volumes of other computer peripherals around the world. The domestic and offshore banking, foreign exchange, financial futures and insurance industries have all shown strong growth in the 1990s.

The US is the nation's largest foreign investor, concentrating on petroleum, chemicals and electronics.

Singapore has a chronically tight labour market which causes rising labour costs. Unemployment averages about 2%. Nearly a fifth of Singapore's workers are immigrants from neighbouring countries. The country strongly encourages local firms to invest abroad and 'regionalise' their activities. More than a quarter of Singapore's investments abroad are in ASEAN countries, principally in Malaysia and Hong Kong. Billions also go to the Netherlands Antilles (a tax haven) and the USA.

The government has given special attention to a number of joint ventures in Indonesia, India, and, most prominently, China. All of these use Singapore's strengths in logistics, planning and management. The largest venture is a 70 sq. km industrial township currently being built by a joint Singapore–China consortium near Suzhou in China. There is also the Batam Industrial Park and Bintan Industrial Estate in Indonesia, the Bangalore Information Technology Park in India, the Wuxi-Singapore Industrial Park in China and many other smaller developments throughout the region.

South Korea

Korea began its economic development in earnest in 1962, having started from scratch at the end of World War II. For more than 30 years it has experienced an annual average growth rate of 8%. This exceptionally good performance is attributed mainly to the effective combination of an abundant, high-quality labour supply with cheap foreign capital and technology, all controlled carefully through centralised government.

Regardless of the currency crisis, these advantages have been diminishing because of changes abroad and at home. Internationally, Korea is experiencing increasing difficulties in overcoming protectionist barriers in its exports to the West and Japan. The obvious solution to the need for new markets, which is economic co-operation between countries in the region, has greatly expanded but in doing so countries with vast sources of cheap labour, in particular China, are emerging as a threat to Korea's exports everywhere in the world.

At home, Korea has gone through a process of democratisation which has led to labour disputes and high wage demands. Between 1983 and 1992 wage increases in manufacturing have been about 19% a year. The liberalisation of the financial markets and the increase in disposable incomes has bought about private overconsumption and speculation.

The chaebol miracle

South Korea is today the 11th largest economy in the world. Its celebrated 'chaebol' system is modelled on that of Japan, its traditional enemy. Japan established its influence in Korea in the last century and formally annexed it in 1910. The Japanese occupation was brutal, but when South Korea achieved independence in 1948, it was naturally to Japan that the new country turned when planning how to industrialise itself. Two methods, in particular, were adopted – aggressive exports and the establishment of huge conglomerates, or 'chaebol' (known as 'keiretsu' in Japan). As with Japan, Korea kept up barriers against the importation of foreign goods.

Unlike keiretsu, the Korean chaebol operates in many industries and has been centrally controlled by the government. The two countries are in competition to some extent. Hyundai and Daewoo, two of the big four chaebol, have had enormous success in shipbuilding, outstripping Japan. Similarly, Korean cars have become a threat to Japanese export markets.

Park Chung Hee, president from 1961 until his assassination in 1979, is regarded as the founder of the country's economic success. A former lieutenant in the imperial Japanese air force, he won power with a military coup, nationalised all the Korean banks and reinforced the chaebol system. His regime was autocratic and austere – leading businessmen were arrested, but then released on the promise to invest their wealth in areas decided on by the government.

The main features of chaebol are:

- They are groups of many companies centred on one holding company. The parent company is usually controlled by one family.
- The top four chaebol have sales of over 40% of the country's GNP.
- Unlike Japanese keiretsu, chaebol do not have their own banks and are thus less independent of government.
- Most chaebol remain overwhelmingly family concerns. It is estimated that about 12% of senior chaebol executives are close relatives of the founders of the companies.

There are four superchaebol.

Hyundai
Hyundai was begun by Chung Ju Yung, in 1947 as a construction firm. The company did not hit the big league until the 1973 oil crisis, when Chung moved into the Gulf and also undertook an ambitious shipbuilding programme. By the late 1980s it had become the world's biggest shipbuilder,

but has recently been overtaken by Daewoo. Shipbuilding has been supported heavily by the government and apparent failures have not been allowed to affect the company. Hyundai, like the other chaebols, is expanding its car production, with plants all over South East Asia, Africa and the Middle East.

Daewoo
Kim Woo Chong, the founder of Daewoo, was born in humble circumstances in 1936 but is now estimated to be worth nearly $2 billion. Daewoo began in 1967 as a textile company; it now employs over 100,000 people and turns over around $60 billion a year. While broadly diversified, Daewoo aims to increase its car production massively. Unlike the other chaebol leaders, Kim has said that he does not want to be succeeded by relatives.

Samsung
Lee Kun Hee, the head of Samsung, has a catchphrase – 'Change everything except your wife'. With labour costs rising, Lee is investing billions in leading edge electronic and biological technologies in the hope that Samsung will prosper in a post semiconductor era. A subsidiary, Samsung Electronics, is a major exporter of televisions, VCRs and white goods. The grandson of Samsung's founder Lee Byung Chul, Lee hopes that Samsung will be one of the world's top car makers by 2010.

Lucky Goldstar Electronics
Lucky Goldstar is owned by Koo Bon Moo, grandson of the founder, and began life as a toothpaste factory in the late 1940s. It became the country's leading chaebol in the 1970s when it had huge success in low cost consumer electrical goods, but now has lapsed back into third place. Koo has bought a majority stake in the American TV manufacturer Zenith and the company is now selling products which compete with big names such as Philips and Siemens.

Taiwan

Once known as Formosa, Taiwan is an island off the coast of China. It became an independent country in 1949 when Chiang Kai Shek brought the remnants of the Kuomintang army to the island, leaving the mainland to the victorious Communists. Tensions between the two regimes have remained active since then and no discussion of the economy of the Republic of China (as the Taiwan government is still named) is intelligible unless the underlying political problem is understood. In the Cold War years the island received massive aid from the USA to bolster it against mainland China's claims to it, and Taiwan enjoyed diplomatic recognition throughout the world until the late 1960s, when China's relations began to improve with the rest of the world. This change resulted in Taiwan's expulsion from the UN in 1971 and the USA ending formal relations with it in 1979.

Although by 1981 very few nations maintained diplomatic relations with Taiwan its economy continued to expand. In 1991 a plan for reunification with mainland China was introduced but relations deteriorated when China held military manoeuvres nearby in the run-up to the island's first direct presidential elections in 1996 and the United States sent the 7th fleet to protect the coast of Taiwan. While the USA no longer formally recognises Taiwan, there is reason to suppose that it will continue to support the island as part of its policy to maintain stability in the Far East.

Taiwan is one of Asia's major industrial economies. About 35% of the workforce is in manufacturing. The island produces electrical and electronic equipment, cement, crude steel, chemicals, refined petroleum, textiles, and plastic items.

Taiwan accounts for 2.1% of the world's trade with 0.4% of its population; it is the world's 18th largest exporter. In recent years GDP growth has been running at an average of 6.5% annually. Official per capita income is around US$12,500, but with a large black economy a more realistic figure might be $20,000. Unemployment is considered high at 2.5%, but is arguably a symptom of Taiwan's maturity as an advanced economy. Personal savings from income is nearly 30%. The Taiwan stock market has been of serious interest to institutional investors since 1996.

Like the other Asian success stories, Taiwan has transformed itself during the post-war era. Once an aid recipient, it is now a donor of aid and an investor in other Asian countries. The United States is Taiwan's largest trading partner, receiving 26% of Taiwan's exports and supplying 21% of its imports. Electronics is Taiwan's most important industrial export sector and is the largest recipient of US investment. This dependency is expected to decrease as Asian markets grow.

President Lee Teng-hui succeeded Chiang Ching-kuo (son of Chiang Kai Shek) in 1988, ushering in an era of liberalisation, politically and economically (nearly 40 years of martial law only ended in 1987). The ruling Kuomintang party now has credible political opponents and press freedoms have been introduced. Relatively low tax rates, a transparent regulatory framework, prudential supervision of banks, a sound legal infrastructure, and a conservative fiscal policy have helped the island's economy remain vigorous. A culture of entrepreneurship has brought a flexible approach to information technology industries where adaptability is vital.

Taiwan cannot afford to take another route; as its government lowers import barriers and external competition increases, it sees further economic liberalisation – and some rapport with China, where it has large light industry investments – as vital to its future.

The economic giant – Japan

Of the countries examined in this chapter, Japan is by far the most economically powerful and mature. Its population is 121 million. Along with North America and Western Europe, Japan is one of the three major industrial complexes of the world.

During the Allied occupation of Japan after World War II, Japan established a democratic self-government and continued its process of rapid modernisation which it began in the late nineteenth century.

Japan's GDP comes mainly from trade, manufacturing, mining and construction (56%) and services (23%). In 1995 the GDP figure was over US$5 **trillion**, with a growth rate of 0.9%. Its per capita GDP was nearly double that of the UK, at $40,897. Japan's major export markets are the USA (30%), Western Europe (14%) and the developing countries (48%). It is the USA's principal ally in Asia and the two interdependent nations co-operate closely in almost all areas; like the USA, it is committed to promoting open international trade across the world, although its own internal markets are heavily protected. Together the US and Japan make up a third of the world's economic output, the alliance compensating somewhat for Japan's traditional unpopularity in the rest of Asia. The US continues to try to increase access to Japan's markets – between 1986 and 1996, US exports to Japan increased from $27 billion to $65 billion. As part of the GATT Uruguay Round agreement Japan agreed in December 1993 to open its rice market, which had historically been closed to foreign rice, and agreed to reduce tariffs on many goods.

Although US investment into Japan has much increased in recent years, foreign investors continue to encounter a range of formal and informal barriers in Japan, and the country accepts a far smaller share of global foreign direct investment than any of its G7 counterparts. After a massive increase in Japanese investment in the US in the 1980s there was a slowdown, but it is currently over $100 billion, compared with around $40 billion from the US to Japan.

Japan's internal problems are beginning to resemble those in the other high income areas. Unemployment is at a post-war high. Traditional norms, such as lifetime employment and keiretsu supplier relationships, are eroding in large part due to globalisation. Foreign criticism of Japan has shifted from its high customs tariffs to the alleged anti-competitive behaviour of its firms with their exclusive supplier/distributor arrangements and domination of particular markets.

Early in 1997, Prime Minister Hashimoto announced that:

'The Japanese socio-economic system, which has sustained the coun-
try over the 50 year post-war period, now has revealed serious limita-
tions. To create a new Japanese socio-economic system suitable for the
21st century, I am promoting reforms particularly in the following six
areas: administrative reform, economic structural reform, financial
system reform, social security reform, fiscal reform, and education re-
form.'

This is not merely a politician's rhetoric; hitherto, Japan has had a 'sponsored capitalism' controlled by the government and what is now being
proposed is to allow private enterprise to take the initiative. Western opinion has been sceptical, but Japanese observers argue that many influential
voices are now emerging in their nation who are no longer willing to toe a
monolithic, totalitarian line. While traditions of internal co-operation are
still highly valued, demands for transparency are now strident.

Conclusion

Globalisation has led to a proliferation of euphemisms – international agencies and diplomats necessarily choose their words carefully to avoid of-
fence, and commerce's rhetoric must also avoid scaring away customers.
To use plainer language, by the middle of 1997, commercial optimism was
buoyant because of East Asia's stupendously good growth rates – within
two generations, whole countries had moved from being peasant socie-
ties (in many cases devastated by unasked-for wars) to being highly educated, high technology arenas where anything seemed – and still seems –
possible. The so-called mature economies apparently have nowhere to go,
and the new-found ability of Asia to take over the world's manufacturing
seemed to offer as much hope to the West as to the East – for the rich West
very evidently cannot afford to pay its own citizens to work in factories.
The collapse of Russian communism and the subsequent rush of the ex-
communist bloc towards capitalism only emphasised the commercial potential of Asia, whose people were actually willing to work and to save –

at root, the twin engines of capitalism. Yet throughout this *fin de siècle* turbulence it has always been evident to informed observers that those Asian countries who comprise the economic 'miracle' are not in any sense carbon copies of Western countries at an earlier stage of development, as the general optimistic atmosphere suggested; they are themselves and are in the globalisation game for their own reasons. When the game seemed to change its rules in the latter half of 1997, the reaction of Asian countries gave strong hints of the turbulence we can expect in the next century – already touted as the 'Pacific century'.

Part 1

Diary of a Disaster

Pre-crisis

The year opened with few clouds in the sky.

In Singapore, in February, ex-Prime Minister Lee Kuan Yew says that the economy will perform better in 1997 than in 1996.

In Thailand, the government forecasts growth of 6.8%. London forex dealers are reported to be uncertain about future levels for the Thai baht because of fears of a major policy change in Thailand affecting exports.

A survey finds that most banks do not regard Hong Kong as the most risky area in South East Asia, despite the coming June 1997 handover to China. Indonesia is thought the most risky, following the political unrest of 1996. The Chinese yuan, the Taiwan dollar and the South Korean won are expected to increase in strength.

In Japan, the major Japanese companies are expecting their profits to rise, with their combined parent pre-tax profits gaining 7.8% in the year ending March 1998.

1997 voted year of the ringgit: analysts see Malaysia's currency as best buy in Asia

International Herald Tribune, 4 January 1997

Thailand

Since the middle of 1995 Thailand's economic growth has shown signs of pressure from serious floods, political unrest and rapidly increasing prices. Growth has continued largely because of an expansion in sales to ASEAN countries and a finance and property boom which has attracted short-term money from abroad.

The discovery that the Bangkok Bank of Commerce's (BBC) bad debts are serious, and suspicions of fraud, shakes confidence in the central bank, the Bank of Thailand, which had given assurances that all was well with BBC. It also emerges that the central bank's governor had received shares from a company while serving in his capacity as a representative of the central bank on the company's Board of Directors.

As volatility in the money markets grows, the central bank tries to dampen down demand at home by maintaining credit controls and high interest rates. It also attempts to reduce Thailand's reliance on short-term foreign capital by, among other actions, introducing tighter restrictions on commercial banks.

Elections in July 1995 were won by a coalition led by Banharn Silpa-archa of the Chart Thai party. Just over a year later the government collapsed amidst corruption scandals. The 1996 election produced another unstable coalition government, led by General Chavalit Yongchaiyudh of the New Aspiration Party (NAP). In an atmosphere of vote-buying and violence, the NAP became the largest party in the 393-member House of Representatives, winning 125 seats against 123 Democrat seats. General Chavalit heads a government similar in membership to the one preceding it and liable to similar difficulties. Business had hoped for the Democrats to win, and the Stock Exchange of Thailand (SET) fell by 5.8% on news of the '96 election result.

March 1997

Monday 3 March

Following problems in the property market, Thai regulators order major changes in banking rules to force lenders to increase their bad loan provisions. They instruct ten finance companies with liquidity problems to increase their capital by more than US$300 million. This leads to a run on the deposits of the ten companies involved.

Later that week, Michel Camdessus, the chief of the International Monetary Fund (IMF), reproaches the Thai financial regulators for lax supervision. He reassures investors, however, by saying 'I don't see any reason for this crisis to develop further'.

The Thai stock exchange (SET) falls all week but recovers on Friday, at which point it is 17% down since the beginning of the year.

Analysts say that data is hard to come by, but estimate that nonperforming loans (mainly in property) could cost banks and finance companies 800 billion baht (US$30.82 billion).

Camdessus says that Thailand is not the only country in the region to lack a developed regulatory framework for its financial markets. 'In many countries in Asia and elsewhere, prudential regulation and supervision have not kept pace with the new complexities of banking business.' He points out that such regulation is all the more necessary when there is big foreign money involved: 'The presence of large capital inflows reduces the room for policy manoeuvre and limits the scope for policy mistakes.'

May 1997

Friday 16 May

The Thai baht hits an 11-year low against the dollar this week as speculators forcefully sell South East Asian currencies. The Thai central bank introduces restrictions on lending to foreign borrowers in an attempt to reduce speculation. Singapore joins Thailand in heavy buying in support of the baht.

'The important thing is that the joint intervention was effective', says Koh Beng Seng, the deputy managing director of the Monetary Authority of Singapore.

The speculators' selling is reported to be caused by growing doubts about the Thai economy and political situation. The Thai stock exchange reaches an 8-year low.

Friday 23 May

The New York Cotton Exchange (NYCE) announces that it will launch futures contracts next month on four South East Asian currencies: the Singapore dollar, the Indonesian rupiah, the Thai baht and the Malaysian ringgit.

There is pressure on Malaysia to internationalise its currency. The NYCE's decision to trade the ringgit contract may compel Bank Negara, the central bank of Malaysia, to approve the ringgit futures trading on the Malaysian Monetary Exchange. Bank Negara is said to fear foreign speculation should the ringgit become an international currency, as has happened with the troubled baht.

An international currency dealer says that there is no reason to fear attacks on the ringgit in the futures market as the central bank is in full control of the cash market. He argues that the volume of trading would be small, but agrees that if futures trading grows, fluctuations there can affect the cash market.

June 1997

Monday 2 June

Cross Border Capital (CBC), an asset allocation adviser in London, ranks 54 currencies in the world, placing the ringgit in fourth place and the Singapore dollar in seventh. It estimates that these two Asian currencies are the most likely to appreciate against the US dollar, while the Philippine peso and Korean won have a considerable devaluation risk.

CBC analyst Mark Clayton says that currencies are measured by three factors: relative liquidity, fundamental balance and sentiment. He regards Malaysia as having a strong fundamental surplus in its long-term cash inflows which are ploughed into the real economy, saying that Malaysia's current account deficit is shrinking rapidly because of strong export growth. CBC ranks Thailand at 44 because its 'fundamental balance' is weak.

Wednesday 18 June

Amnuay Viravan, the Thai finance minister, resigns his post. Prime Minister Chavalit promises that 'We will never devalue the baht'.

Friday 20 June

Thanong Bidaya becomes Thailand's new minister of finance.

Wednesday 25 June

Thanong Bidaya goes in person to the central bank, the Bank of Thailand, to demand detailed figures. He discovers that most of the country's foreign exchange reserves (US$30 billion) are tied up in forward exchange contracts. The country's true foreign reserves are only just over US$1 billion.

He also discovers that the Financial Institutions Development Fund (FIDF), which is controlled by the central bank, has lent over US$8 billion to Thailand's troubled financial firms. The country's largest finance institution, Finance One, has received US$1.4 billion alone from the FIDF in the last three months.

Later that day it is leaked that the FIDF will not buy new shares in Finance One, as it had promised earlier.

Friday 27 June

Finance One closes down, along with another 15 finance companies.

July 1997 – the crisis begins

Wednesday 2 July

The Thai baht's long-standing peg to the US dollar is removed by finance minister Thanong in order to prevent the country defaulting on international debts. This is a *de facto* devaluation, since the baht is now 'floating' and headed downwards.

The Bank of Thailand says that International Monetary Fund (IMF) officials are advising it on new monetary policy measures. Deputy central bank governor Chaiyawat Wibulsawasdi says that 'the IMF is briefing the bank on the implementation of the short-term monetary policies after the adoption of new floating foreign exchange system'.

Bank Negara steps in a second day to shore up ringgit: Bangkok stocks surge another 8.6%

Business Times (Singapore), 4 July 1997

Friday 4 July

For two days Malaysia's central bank, Bank Negara, has heavily supported the ringgit following selling of the currency as short-term interest rates fell; Malaysia's one-week money market rates were as low as 5.15% (for one-week money market rates) compared with 6.03% one week ago.

Tuesday 8 July

Bank Negara sells between US$1 billion (S$1.44 billion) and US$2 billion in Kuala Lumpur, New York and London to support the ringgit, hurting speculators.

Wednesday 9 July

Bank Negara warns foreign funds that it will take stern measures to stem speculation. The strategy seems to be to prop up the ringgit and raise interest rates through market intervention. It has not ordered local banks to stop selling ringgit to offshore banks, which it did in the 1980s.

The Philippine central bank increases the overnight inter-bank borrowing rate for the fourth time since the Thai devaluation, pushing it to 32%, its highest ever.

Thursday 10 July

Malaysia's overnight inter-bank lending rate rises more than 500%, to 50% from yesterday's 9%, the highest rate in over four years.

Friday 11 July

Malaysia's acting Prime Minister Anwar Ibrahim says that international funds speculating heavily against the ringgit do not understand the region. Finance minister Datuk Seri Anwar says that the ringgit should not come under undue pressure because Malaysia has political stability and good economic fundamentals.

Says another minister, 'We have been telling people we are not Thailand, but they still believe we are ... our economic fundamentals are good and the 8 per cent growth target this year will be met.' When he is asked why local funds were not supporting the stock market after foreign funds left in March, he replies: 'This is not really a mature market. We understand the market, we should take the lead, not foreigners. In fact, the market now offers an opportunity to buy.'

Growth in huge infrastructure projects, such as the Bakun hydroelectric dam and extensions to Kuala Lumpur International Airport, is officially not expected to slow.

Currency traders describe Bank Negara's actions as a classic 'bear-trap', pointing out that bears on the ringgit felt safe until the overnight rate shot up yesterday. Speculators who sold ringgit which they didn't possess last week would now have to borrow at much higher interest rates when their bets became due for payment.

Thursday 24 July

The Thai baht sinks to a record low of 32.70 to the US dollar.

Friday 25 July

Thai Finance Minister Thanong Bidaya is to present a plan to the cabinet on the 5 of August outlining measures to stabilise the baht, increase liquidity, improve the property and finance industries and make tax collection more efficient.

International bankers are still bearish, and with the power to lend to Thai businesses, their opinion matters. Hitoshi Komasaka, general manager of the Japanese Sanwa Bank's branch in Bangkok, says 'I'm looking for an announcement from Dr Thanong within the next two weeks, and that might be that they are willing to accept some assistance from the IMF, the Japanese government, or some other foreign government.'

The Japanese government and banks are reported to have made their help conditional on a Thai deal with the IMF. The Thai government appears to be reluctant to include the IMF in a rescue package. Thailand last had a program with the IMF in 1985.

US gives thumbs up to news of IMF–Thailand talks

Reuters, 28 July 1997

Monday 28 July

US Deputy Treasury Secretary Lawrence Summers says 'We welcome the dialogue between Thailand and the International Monetary Fund as a constructive step and will be following it closely. The United States has a strong stake in financial stability and growth throughout the developing world.'

Thai officials agree publicly that they are about to consider asking for an IMF loan.

August 1997

Friday 1 August

As US pressure on Thailand to make a deal with the IMF continues, an IMF official gives his anonymous perspective; referring to the IMF's criticisms of Thai economic policies in June and a subsequent refusal by Thailand to allow publication of an account of the discussion, he says 'That should tell you something: The Thais thumbed their nose at us all along.' The official points out Japan's refusal to help without an IMF deal and harks back to a speech in November 1996 by the IMF's chief, Michel Camdessus, warning that despite their high growth, South East Asian countries faced new risks to their stability. 'It had no effect beyond making the Asians angry,' says the IMF official. 'They thought they could manage on their own.'

The IMF had instituted an 'early warning system' earlier in the year to help prevent problems in emerging economies. The countries concerned were encouraged to provide markets with as much economic information as possible. The IMF was to increase its monitoring for signs of trouble and made its lending procedures easier so that borrowing countries could obtain loans more quickly. It also started to publish details of the countries it monitors if the country concerned agreed – which Thailand did not.

Sunday 3 August

Dr Mahathir Mohamad, Prime Minister of Malaysia, who has been publicly castigating foreign currency speculators for some time, was asked to respond to a report that George Soros, the currency trader, had asked to meet him to discuss his allegations. 'Well, I will certainly consider it. We'll find out what he wants to explain,' he answers.

The Malaysian government announces further restrictions on local banks' lending to currency dealers in an attempt to reduce attacks on the ringgit. Since the Thai baht floated on 2 July, the ringgit has fallen by 4% against the dollar.

Tuesday 5 August

Malaysian shares have their largest fall in one day since 1995 following poor trade deficit figures.

Friday 8 August

Malaysian Prime Minister Mahathir Mohamad says that the government will not continue to defend the ringgit, remarking that 'We're satisfied with the ringgit's current level, even if the value falls, we will do nothing because we're confident that it will recover'. He opines that while traders such as George Soros can interfere with currencies 'no country is safe'.

There are worries that loans in Malaysia are not going to productive industries and doubts that new lending restrictions will actually slow growth, since the system offers loopholes and exemptions.

Monday 11 August

The ringgit continues to fall without support from Malaysia's central bank, apparently confirming Dr Mahathir's remarks on Friday. Other South East Asian currencies also fall – including the baht, in spite of a promise of an IMF sponsored package of US$16 billion in loans to Thailand. There is talk of 'capital flight' from Malaysia.

Thursday 14 August

The Indonesian rupiah floats.

Friday 15 August

Dr Mahathir Mohamad maintains that Malaysia's growth will still be at 8% this year, and encouraged local funds 'to flex their muscles' so that the market would not be too dependent on foreign funds, most of which had left the local stock exchange. He says that Malaysia has learned to be flexible in these conditions: 'As we move into the information age where national boundaries will not be able to protect us, we will be exposed to powerful foreign predators who may not be too sympathetic to our well-being.'

Monday 18 August

Standard & Poor's lowers Malaysia's credit-rating outlook, saying that slower economic growth could harm the country's banking system; 'With the authorities under pressure to curb rapid credit growth, and the economy likely to slow further as a result, asset quality problems likely will surface in the banking system.' The rating change implies that borrowing abroad will become more expensive. S & P expects Malaysia's growth to be 7% in 1997, a 'moderate' slowdown.

Thursday 21 August

Standard & Poor's downgrades its credit-rating outlook for five of the largest banks in Indonesia and Malaysia. It prophesies that further currency falls could lead to more bad debts. The banks involved are Malayan Banking Bhd. (Malaysia's largest), Arab-Malaysian Merchant Bank Bhd, and, in Indonesia, PT Bank Negara Indonesia, PT Bank Danamon and PT Bank Umum Nasional. While the actual credit ratings do not change, S & P cuts the outlook rating from 'stable' to 'negative'.

Saturday 23 August

This week the World Bank is reported as offering to arrange a meeting between Malaysian Prime Minister Dr Mahathir Mohamad and George Soros. Dr Mohamad says he will not meet Soros and that the World Bank has no business arranging such a meeting. The Malaysian press is critical of Soros, arguing that while the trader asserts that he is concerned with human rights in developing countries and has set up foundations to help victims of human rights abuses, he has no compunction about speculating in the currencies of those nations. Soros, however, has denied speculating in ASEAN currencies.

Tuesday 26 August

The South Korean won hits a record low against the dollar. The Bank of Korea (BOK) is forced to intervene, depleting foreign exchange reserves, and lends money to troubled banks. So far this year six South Korean conglomerates have become insolvent.

Thursday 28 August

Malaysia ends its special 100,000 ringgit tax on property purchases by foreigners which was intended to keep prices within reach of Malaysians. This is not expected to affect the crashing property market.

The finance minister says 'I will have a definite plan to deal with the current account deficit within several weeks' and that the country will 'substantially' reduce the deficit, using 'very tough measures'. June's trade deficit was 2.8 billion ringgit (US$1 billion).

Prime Minister Mahathir is reported to have asked Malaysian state-run pension funds like the Employees Provident Fund and Permodolan Nasional Bhd. to buy shares on Friday. The PM repeated his charge that George Soros, was behind the market problems, saying he had evidence.

Restrictions aimed at preventing short-selling are introduced which ban the short-selling of any of the 100 shares in the Malaysian exchange's composite index. The market drops by 8%.

Southeast Asia's tiger economies lose growl: stocks plunged and currencies collapsed against the US dollar as weaknesses arose, but leaders remain confident

The Vancouver Sun, 30 August 1997

Friday 29 August

Stock markets across Asia are dropping as Western fund managers sell their investments. It is the ninth consecutive week that they have done so.

'There is a complete loss of confidence in the region,' says Tan Min Lan, senior economist in Singapore for Merrill Lynch. 'We have large sell orders from our clients who want to cut back their exposure to Asia.'

In Japan, the market drops on the news that former vice-president of Yamaichi Securities Co. was being questioned by Tokyo prosecutors in a widening payoff scandal.

Fund managers' doubts are widely said to have been exacerbated by politicians' attacks on foreign speculators, in particular the remarks of Dr Mahathir. 'It basically turns the Kuala Lumpur Exchange into the least competent market in the region', says a foreign analyst in Malaysia's capital.

Peter Churchhouse, the chief regional strategist of the investment bank Morgan Stanley, is said by Reuters to have announced that Morgan Stanley had suspended trading in all Malaysian stocks, saying 'There are enough problems in these markets as it is without authorities changing the rules of the game in these sorts of ways'.

Analysts and traders warn that the support of the ringgit, rupiah and other currencies is unsustainable, and predict severe drops soon.

Hong Kong has suffered less than other markets, its currency still firmly tied to the US dollar. There are worries about the 'red chip' mainland Chinese companies now listed in Hong Kong. Singapore has dropped a little, and its blue chips are expected to be affected by problems in neighbouring Malaysia.

In spite of the chaos in the financial markets, the Western multinationals have no intention of closing down their operations in the region; Ford Motor Co., Coca-Cola Co. and Texas Instruments Inc., among others, all confirm this publicly. A spokesman for Texas Instruments says 'There is a great deal of irrational panic surrounding events in Southeast Asia now, and most of it is misplaced. The miracle is not over yet.'

In Thailand next week the parliament will begin a debate on a new draft constitution. Big crowds are expected to gather outside the parliament, building. Those in favour of the new constitution say that it will clean up elections and reduce vote buying. Those against include heads of villages and districts who help organise vote buying for politicians. The IMF's loan earlier this month has helped with the country's finances, but a minister, referring to turmoil in neighbouring countries, says 'If the internal factors improve while external ones do not, the country's economy will continue to suffer'. There is a new acceptance in Thailand that currency stability is more important than trying to keep a high rate.

Analysts predict political problems in Indonesia. Indonesia's only state-owned bank providing housing loans for people earning low-incomes suspends its lending.

Sunday 31 August

Malaysians celebrate 40 years of independence. In a speech marking the independence anniversary, Prime Minister Mahathir Mohamad continues to accuse speculators of attempting to destroy the economy, saying 'Today we have seen how easily foreigners deliberately bring down our economy by undermining our currency and stock exchange. What we have worked for in the past 40 years can be destroyed by them in a matter of weeks.' Mahathir is 71 and has been PM since 1981. In the speech he reverses earlier forecasts and admits that the 8% growth rate may not be achieved.

Describing currency traders as 'ferocious animals', he says that 'If we do not strive to protect our independence, directly or indirectly, colonialists will return to colonize us'.

Commentators point out that the Prime Minister's rhetoric is for home consumption – it is not intended for the West. Malaysia's planned Multimedia Supercorridor, an information technology 'city' near Kuala Lumpur, has received firm commitments from Microsoft and other important IT companies, evidence of Malaysia's drive to attract foreign 'knowledge workers' to the country.

September 1997

City: Malaysia accuses IMF of support for speculators

The Daily Telegraph, 1 September 1997

Wednesday 3 September

Indonesia says it will delay major infrastructure projects, curb luxury imports and increase exports.

Thursday 4 September

Malaysia threatens to use its tough anti-subversion law to arrest those who 'sabotage' its economy and announces that it will postpone important construction projects including the Bakun dam, a 6 billion US dollar scheme. The ban on short-selling is lifted, however.

The region's troubled currencies – the Malaysian ringgit, Philippine peso, Thai baht and Indonesian rupiah – all make new record lows.

Sunday 7 September

Deputy Prime Minister Korn Dabbaransi of Thailand echoes Dr Mahathir's views, announcing that finance ministers from ASEAN countries will stand together at the annual meetings of the International Monetary Fund and the World Bank in Hong Kong this month. Dr Mahathir has called on the world community to outlaw currency manipulation – but not speculation.

Thailand is to host a meeting of Asian and European finance ministers on 18 and 19 September in Bangkok. The ministers will then fly to Hong Kong for the IMF–World Bank annual gathering.

Sunday 14 September

Dr Mahathir meets foreign fund managers as part of his government's efforts to reassure nervous investors about Malaysia's economic policies. He concedes that Malaysia may have made mistakes in trying to prevent the stock market selling.

Analysts who were present say they are impressed and reassured by Dr Mahathir. Although they are happy with the country's reforms they are still uncertain about growth prospects, but agree that growth will be 'above 6.5%'.

Thursday 18 September

Yaohan Japan Corporation files for reorganisation under Japanese bankruptcy law. It has suffered from over-rapid expansion overseas and by deregulation at home.

Friday 19 September

At the two-day Asia–Europe Finance Ministers' meeting (18–19 September), Malaysian Deputy Prime Minister Datuk Seri Anwar Ibrahim says that developing nations may not push for more reforms in the World Trade Organisation liberalisation package if a mechanism to protect emerging markets from excessive speculation is not put in place. He argues that for the path to liberalisation to unfold smoothly, emerging markets must feel protected and not cheated, and calls for the IMF to work out a regulatory framework along the lines of the existing prudential regulations on the banking industry, for hedge funds and investment houses.

Anwar is not opposing the concept of liberalisation which he agrees has brought tremendous benefits to emerging countries.

The response of European delegates is said to be 'muted'.

Saturday 20 September

In Hong Kong, Prime Minister Dr Mahathir Mohamad, makes a much-awaited speech at the IMF–World Bank meeting to an audience of international financiers and civil servants. Pointing out that forex trading is 20 times larger than trading in goods or services, he says that it should be stopped as it is 'unnecessary, unproductive and totally immoral'. He describes currency trading as 'secretive and shady' and claims that market turmoil in the region is 'a move by Western industrialised nations to keep Asia poor'.

Dr Mahathir points out that there is no such thing as an entirely free market and that even the European Commission, which seems to believe in the free market and is strongly advocating it, does not practise it in its entirety.

Sunday 21 September

At the IMF–World Bank annual meetings in Hong Kong George Soros attacks Dr Mahathir, saying 'Dr Mahathir is a menace to his own country … Dr Mahathir's suggestion yesterday to ban currency trading is so inappropriate that it does not deserve serious consideration.' He asserts that 'I have been subjected to all kinds of false and vile accusations by Dr Mahathir. He is using me as a scapegoat to cover up his own failure. He is playing to a domestic audience, and he couldn't get away with it if he and his ideas were subject to the discipline of independent media inside Malaysia. Unfortunately, anything I say here won't reach the local audience because he controls the media. If he didn't, he wouldn't be able to grandstand the way he does.'

Soros goes on to argue that freedom of information is of critical importance at this time, and that ASEAN governments have a responsibility to make sure that the poor people of Burma are helped. Later he denies that he has been involved in speculative attacks on regional currencies. He rejects the idea of 'Asian values' promoted by Dr Mahathir: 'The emphasis on Asian values has served as a convenient pretext for resisting democratic aspirations. Autocratic regimes which restrict free speech and foster corruption cannot last forever.'

Mahathir has refused to meet Soros face to face at the World Bank meeting. Instead they have addressed each other indirectly through speeches.

An IMF committee announces that it is seeking new powers to encourage member states to lift constraints on the movement of investment capital in and out of their markets.

Later at the conference Chinese Vice-Premier Zhu Rongji promises that China would again offer tax breaks to foreign investors for importing capital goods. 'China will reintroduce certain policy incentives – that is, tax breaks – towards the import of equipment needed for the foreign-invested projects that meet requirements', Zhu says, and receives warm applause from the audience.

Zhu explains that the projects eligible under the new scheme must conform to the industrial policies of China and bring with them new technology instead of repetitive construction at a low technological level. China used to offer breaks in tariffs and value-added tax to encourage foreign investment but ended the incentives on 1 April 1996. He says that a principal reason for the cancellation was the government's worry about the reduction of revenue income when China cut its import tariff from 35.9% to 23%.

'It is unreasonable to make excessive demands on China, which is a developing country', he says. 'China's entry into WTO will benefit not only China's economic development, but also world economic growth.'

Regarding the banking and insurance sector, Zhu comments that it will take time for China to open the market fully to foreign institutions. 'We will surely offer you licences to open branches in China, but be patient.'

Monday 22 September

Malaysian shares and currency drops further. The chief of a major trading bank says 'They don't seem to be speculators but genuine sellers. They just want to cover their foreign currency liabilities on fears that their access to offshore markets could be cut off.'

Most ASEAN currencies fall. Against the US dollar, the Singapore dollar hits 1.5300 (compared to 1.5180 on Friday), the Thai baht ends at 36.40 (35.80), while the Indonesian rupiah again broke above 3000 to close at 3040 (2970). Only the Philippine peso closes stronger at 33.15 (33.80).

Markets gulp after Mahathir remarks

International Herald Tribune, 23 September 1997

Wednesday 24 September

Malaysia's ambitious Multimedia Supercorridor (MSC) has not been postponed. Japan's NTT says that it will invest M$64 million (US$21.3 million) over the next three years in R&D in the MSC. NTT's president, Jun-ichiro Miyazu, says 'NTT–MSC's two major areas of concentration will be R&D and communication services for corporate customers, making use of Malaysia's leadership position in Asia and its multi-ethnic characteristics', and that NTT had high regard for the MSC because Malaysia was the first country to come up with concrete plans for investing in the burgeoning multimedia industry.

Ericsson Hewlett-Packard Telecommunications (Ericsson HP) also says it will use the MSC as its regional hub, hoping for 20–30% of its global sales revenue from South East Asia.

Thursday 25 September

Standard & Poor's cuts its long-term ratings outlook for Malaysia again, saying that the country's credit growth is 'unsustainable'. This will raise the country's cost of borrowing. S & P referred to 'profligate' lending to the property industry in Malaysia as a key problem. It also says that the investment boom, which is more than 40% of Malaysia's gross domestic product, was excessive, and that there is 'evident reluctance' by the government to stop it.

Rumours of a collapse at Malaysia Borneo Finance Ltd were denied by the central bank, but hundreds of people lined up to withdraw money from their accounts there.

The Taiwan government says it has spent US$1.4 billion to defend its currency since 1 August, bringing its foreign-currency reserves to a nine-month low of $87.79 billion. Analysts comment that Taiwan has been able to protect itself from the currency turmoil amongst its neighbours.

Falling value of ringgit may worsen Johor's labour woes: states adopt measures to cut costs

Singapore Straits Times, 26 September 1997

Friday 26 September

Malaysians are seeking jobs in Singapore because of the weak ringgit. Meanwhile foreigners, including many Singaporeans, are shopping in Malaysia to take advantage of low prices.

Nick Douch, emerging markets specialist at Barclays Bank in London, says 'Attention has been focused on short sellers aiming to gain from the currency's decline, but the real reason for the slide is that holders who bought the currency and investments before the crisis are trying to get out in an illiquid market'. There is 'anecdotal and actual evidence that the portfolio reallocation out of the region has not yet been completed as investors continue to reassess risk against reward in the Asia–Pacific region'.

He points out that local companies are underhedged and importers and borrowers of foreign currencies are also trying to cut their exposure by buying dollars, and predicts that the crisis will lead to a 'pronounced dislocation of macroeconomic stability' in Malaysia and the region. Inflation is likely to accelerate.

Malaysia takes the region's currency crisis to the United Nations General Assembly, repeating that assistance from the developed countries will be needed if developing countries are not to lose faith in the globalisation process. Foreign Minister Datuk Seri Abdullah Ahmad Badawi says 'The positive response of the developed countries is especially important to maintain the continued commitment and confidence of developing countries on globalisation, on which most of international free trade depends. Such rampant speculation or manipulation of hedge funds in the currency and equity markets of developing countries at a time when they are still feeling their way around in a world of fierce global competition would trigger off a defensive reflex on the part of the affected countries, thereby arousing anti-liberalisation sentiments which would be detrimental to free trade ... in an interdependent world, the crisis warrants the prompt action of the multilateral financial institutions such as the World Bank and the International Monetary Fund, and of the developed countries which should assist the affected economies of East Asia in overcoming the effects of this excessive manipulation and preventing its recurrence.'

Currency crisis taken to UN stage

Business Times (Malaysia), 27 September 1997

Monday 29 September

US Treasury Secretary Robert Rubin returns from a 10-day trip in Asia. 'We can properly be faulted', he says, 'for vastly underinvesting in our relationships with Chinese officials up and down the line. It's no surprise that we keep having such a hard time understanding each other.'

US civil servants say that Japan may now try to regain influence in the region which they have lost during their own recession and banking crisis. Japan is making a proposal for a special fund to rescue Asian nations. Its banks have lent billions of dollars to build many of the projects throughout Asia that are now in trouble. Rubin is said to be against this proposal. He has been well received in China and claims that the US is back at the centre of diplomacy in the region.

In Thailand, analysts think that the country will be able to maintain its foreign reserves above US$23.5 billion, a lower limit set by the IMF, following loans from the Japanese Export–Import Bank, the IMF and a billion dollar currency swap deal with Singapore.

October 1997

Wednesday 1 October

The troubled Asian currencies – the ringgit, rupiah and peso – continue to fall. The baht and Singapore dollar drop less severely.

Supporting Dr Mahathir's continuing campaign, Thai Deputy Finance Minister Chaovarat Charnvirakul says 'The so-called Asian Monetary Fund, if agreed and set up, will be a major step forward in regional monetary cooperation'.

Earlier in the week Dr Mahathir told an audience in Chile, referring to forex speculators, that 'If we cannot stop currency trading, we should at least try to regulate them'.

Tuesday 7 October

Finance minister Richard Hu tells the Singapore Parliament that growth in the region may slow next year, saying that although 'so far the regional currency crisis has had only a small impact on the Singapore economy … in the longer term, the impact will depend on how quickly the regional economies recover and resume their normal growth.'

He illustrates how the Singapore dollar has appreciated strongly against other currencies in the region: 28.9% against the Thai baht; 39.2% against the Indonesian rupiah, and 19.9% against the Malaysian ringgit – although it has fallen against the US dollar, German mark, British pound, Japanese yen and Hong Kong dollar.

Hu said the Monetary Authority favoured the gradual introduction of the Singapore dollar in international trade but that this 'would not be done at a pace which would cause destabilisation' to the currency.

In Japan the pharmaceutical wholesale industry is in crisis. Three of the ten big wholesalers are expected to report operating losses for the year. There are estimates that of the 270 firms currently in the business, only 100 will survive the next two years.

Wednesday 8 October

Dr Mahathir announces that his government is preparing proposals on how to stop the manipulation of Asian currencies. These will be presented to the IMF. He says that 'One of [the proposals] is sure to be that we must have a specific market where currency traders can register themselves and get a set number. If they want to trade, they go there and we know who is trading, where the money comes from, how much credit they get from the bank. We must know all this because only then can we trade. Here, we trade with someone we do not know, he disappears just like that, like a ghost, then it is completely hidden.'

Currency traders said it would be impossible to regulate foreign exchange trading. At present only 5% of the ringgit is traded locally.

Friday 10 October

Dr Mahathir says he suspects that there may be a Jewish 'agenda' behind recent attacks on his country's currency and stock markets. 'We are Muslims, and the Jews are not happy to see Muslims progress. We may suspect that they have an agenda, but we do not want to accuse them.' He is reported as saying that the government was not blaming any Jewish conspiracy for the speculative attacks but that the people who were speculating were Jews and Mr Soros is, incidentally, a Jew.

Analysts say that these remarks are intended to please constituents in the hard-line Malaysian state of Terengganu, where he was speaking.

The ringgit is rising on hopes that the forthcoming budget will restore international confidence in the country's economy.

Singapore dollar getting ready to take the world

South China Morning Post, 10 October 1997

Monday 13 October

On the weekend, Dr Mahathir says that his comments on Jews have been misinterpreted. 'I only made a statement, but the press went on to say that I was accusing the Jews. We cannot make wild accusations ... The Jews are a very strong race. They are the strongest race in the world.'

The chief of the World Trade Organization (WTO) will visit Malaysia later this month to confirm that the country will not tighten controls on currency trading.

Thursday 16 October

Following a poor response, the New York Cotton Exchange (NYCE) calls off its scheme to list futures contracts in four Asian currencies. Since it first offered contracts in the Thai baht, the Indonesian rupiah and the Malaysian ringgit in July, trading volume has been dismally low. In September all the business that was done was 86 contracts in the ringgit. In August, there were five ringgit contracts and none at all in the baht and the rupiah. The Singapore dollar was to be introduced this month.

The reason is evidently the falls in the value of the currencies; under existing rules, profits can be booked only in the currency being traded against the US dollar, which means that a profit booked on a three-month ringgit contract, for example, could be meaningless because the ringgit may have dropped against the dollar by the time the contract ends. The exchange hopes to change the rules so that speculators can book profits in the US dollar for trades in the ASEAN currencies.

The Bank of Japan (BOJ) is in discussion with several Asian banks about a scheme to allow other Asian central banks to borrow yen in a crisis by selling their holdings of Japanese government bonds to the BOJ. These would be sold under repurchase agreements to ensure that the bonds would be bought back later. The BOJ says that the scheme would be used to fix short-term problems only.

Commentators say that the fact that the scheme will be denominated in yen indicates Japan's desire to play a more dominant role in East Asia and its fears that a single currency in the European Union could reduce yen usage.

'We are doing this for the purpose of strengthening facilities for yen investment and boosting use of the yen – we want to make the yen more attractive', a senior Bank of Japan official says.

Friday 17 October

The Malaysian government announces a budget discouraging investment in construction and industries that rely heavily on imports, and designed to stimulate information technology and services.

Finance Minister Anwar confirms the postponement of several large infrastructure projects, including the Bakun hydroelectric dam and a bridge across the Strait of Malacca which is to join peninsular Malaysia with Indonesia. The total cost of these projects is thought to be US$20 billion.

The budget highlights Malaysian concerns that they are becoming uncompetitive. 'We must compete aggressively with low-cost producers in countries like China and Vietnam,' says Mr Anwar. The move to knowledge-based industries is an attempt to move up the 'value chain'. Incentives include US$37.5 million for special schools that will teach computer skills and tax rebates on home computer purchases.

The markets are disappointed and the ringgit slides.

Monday 20 October

In Malaysia, demonstrators are proclaiming their support for the Prime Minister, Dr Mahathir. The country, with a population of only 21 million, seems unified, with even the opposition leader, Lim Kit Siang, emphasising that his Democratic Action Party was not calling for Dr Mahathir to step down in proposing last week that a vote of confidence be considered in Parliament.

The worldwide press attention that the Prime Minister's summer-long controversial remarks have brought is flattering for a small country, even though foreign press comment on Dr Mahathir has tended to be negative. Informed criticisms tend to be based on the country's economics; the key data are:

Malaysia	1997	1998	1999 (forecast)
Real GDP growth, %	7.0	6.9	5.0
Private consumption, %	6.2	5.0	4.0
Gross domestic investment, %	8.0	6.0	3.0
Consumer price inflation, %, annual average	3.8	4.3	3.7
3-month inter-bank rate, % p.a.	9.4	8.5	7.5
GDP, US$ bn	90.1	89.8	99.0
GDP per head, US$	4240	4120	4450
Trade balance, US$ bn	2.9	3.9	4.6
Current-account balance, US$ bn	−6.1	−3.9	−3.2
Exchange rate, M$:US$	2.63	2.83	2.70

Positive signs include:

- An increase in confidence-building measures. This seems likely to be forthcoming, as the government has already put some in place to prevent further overheating of the economy. The shelving of many infrastructure projects will help. Government ministries have had their budgets trimmed by 2%.
- Infrastructure projects which commentators say will help growth are the Multimedia Super Corridor, the Commonwealth Games 1998 and the building of more highways.
- Wage pressure should lessen as the economy slows.
- The current oversupply of property will help to make the country competitive as a place to locate, and new restrictions on banks which prevent them from making more than 20% of their loans for property development will stop another unhealthy boom.

From the point of view of foreign analysts, worrying factors include:

- The so-called 'haze' caused by pollution from forest fires in Indonesia. Almost all of the country is currently covered in a heavy smog, causing health problems, damaging crops and frightening tourists away.
- The banking sector is overextended and bad loans are expected to rise from last year's 3.9%.
- A collapse in consumer demand.
- A stock market drop of 40% since January.

Tuesday 21 October

In South Korea, the won hits a record low as the central bank gives up supporting the currency. 'Companies rushed to buy dollars to secure funds for import payments and banks tried to cover their short positions', a Chase Manhattan dealer says, but then asserts that there will not be a serious won crisis because of adequate central bank reserves and tight foreign exchange regulations.

Friday 24 October

In Singapore inflation is rising because of increasing transport costs, despite the appreciation of the currency against those of its neighbours.

Senior Minister Lee Kuan Yew tells US businessmen in Boston that the Singapore dollar was being allowed to ease to help maintain the island's competitiveness against its neighbours.

Sunday 26 October

In Kuala Lumpur, demonstrators burn an effigy of George Soros.

Monday 27 October

Following Lee Kuan Yew's statements on Friday, the Singapore dollar drops.

In Australia, universities are suffering from a decrease in the number of enrolments from South East Asia, hurting a 3 billion US dollar industry. One of the key regional markets for Australian universities is Malaysia. Fees have risen by nearly 40%.

November 1997

Monday 3 November

The Bank of Japan (BOJ) works with the monetary authorities in Singapore and Indonesia to support the rupiah.

Sanyo goes under; convoy system ends

Asahi Evening News, 4 November 1997.

Sanyo Securities becomes the first brokerage in Japan to seek court protection from creditors since World War II. This underlines the decline of the Finance Ministry's protective 'convoy system', through which troubled financial firms have been assisted by others in the past. This time, major life insurers, banks and brokerages refused to bail out Sanyo, which got into trouble during Tokyo's market slide over the last few months. In common with many other Japanese institutions, Sanyo has large bad debts from property lending.

Tuesday 4 November

Japanese Prime Minister Ryutaro Hashimoto says 'The objective was to stabilise markets in the whole of Asia. Intervention was the method chosen as the most appropriate means in the Indonesian situation.'

Japan says it is determined to play a major role in trying to prevent a currency slide throughout Asia. Finance Minister Hiroshi Mitsuzuka repeats that his country will give support for the economic rehabilitation package for Indonesia put together by the IMF, the World Bank and the Asia Development Bank. Indonesia has been promised a bailout package totalling US$40 billion.

Observers say that the currency crisis might spread to Japan where recently there have been signs that its economic recovery has ground to a halt. Almost 40% of Japanese exports depend on Asian markets.

Friday 7 November

In Hong Kong the stock market slumps along with property prices.

In Korea the won drops by 7% against the dollar. 'The won's tumble raises concerns that another Asian financial crisis may be emerging', Mr Tsao Chung-ping of Ting Kong Securities tells Reuters.

The baht, ringgit, rupiah and Singapore dollar remain firm.

Tuesday 11 November

South Korea's foreign reserves of about $30 billion are 'much less than those of the other three tigers, so that's making them a little bit more vulnerable than Singapore, Hong Kong or Taiwan', says a trader. 'Basically the won pullback has been on the back of intervention by the central bank. There was also some profit-taking.'

Singapore rules out intervention in the slumping property market. 'We are monitoring the situation very closely and studying the various options of what to do if the market takes a sharp downturn', says National Development Minister Lim Hong Kiang on TV. 'There's no way the government can influence the market forces in terms of the prices that go up or go down. We have no fixed or pre-conceived price levels. We will let the market decide the price levels.'

Thursday 13 November

There is speculation that South Korea's banks are heading for collapse.

Friday 14 November

Japan says its economy has arrived at a standstill. 'We can't agree with the view that the economy has entered a recession,' says an official. 'We used a more accurate expression, because the economic recovery seems to be coming to a temporary halt.'

Monday 17 November

French President Jacques Chirac says 'The excessive speculation by some currency traders should be brought under control', after meeting Prime Minister Mahathir Mohamad in Malaysia. 'In other words, we have to find prudential rules to avoid the law of the jungle, and this is in everybody's interest.'

The French leader says he supports the IMF's study to find ways to control excessive currency speculation. The IMF is preparing a study of currency trading. Mahathir and Chirac say that the Group of 15 (G15) developing countries should be represented at meetings of the Group of Seven (G7) industrialised nations.

The G7 is made up of Britain, Canada, France, Germany, Italy, Japan and the United States. The G15 members are Algeria, Argentina, Brazil, Chile, Egypt, Indonesia, India, Jamaica, Kenya, Malaysia, Mexico, Nigeria, Peru, Senegal, Venezuela and Zimbabwe.

In Japan, Hokkaido Takushoku Bank is the latest in a growing list of bank failures because of bad debts. It is one of the nation's ten biggest commercial banks. Government ministers say all deposits at Hokkaido Takushoku will be protected.

Wednesday 19 November

Stock markets in London and continental Europe drop in reaction to the Japanese stock market's dramatic 5.29% fall overnight. Economists say that Korean problems and instability in Japan are of increasing concern.

Friday 21 November

Australia offers to help Korea if Seoul asks the IMF for financial assistance. Korea is Australia's second largest trading partner (after Japan).

Korea is thought to need around US$100 billion, which is much larger than Thailand's US$17 billion aid package.

Monday 24 November

Malaysia's special envoy to the United Nations, Datuk Abdullah Ahmad, says that the international community wrongly perceives Asia's financial problems. 'Countries in the region are lumped into one instead of being looked at individually, and this is a first mistake', he says, pointing out that even the chief of the IMF Michel Camdessus had cited Malaysia as a good example of where the government was aware of the challenges of managing the pressures that result from high growth and maintaining a sound financial system. He says that Camdessus had described its economy as 'solid and prudently managed'.

Abdullah makes the salient point that, only six months ago, Thailand, Indonesia, Malaysia and Singapore were widely pictured as nearly miraculous engines of endless growth, and that now they are being portrayed as weak.

Tuesday 25 November

A row erupts in Japan after its finance ministry claims it had not been aware of an estimated 200 billion yen (US$2.54 billion) in off-the-book debts hidden by the insolvent Yamaichi Securities in dummy companies.

Nihon Keizai Shimbun, Japan's most influential business daily, said in a commentary on Monday that Yamaichi's hidden debts had been an 'open secret' on the market after it was found to have illegally compensated clients for investment losses in 1991: 'If the prime minister really had not received any report at the time, there is nothing more shameful. It means the government has absolutely no crisis management.'

Korea seeks IMF aid to help meet more than US$20 billion worth of foreign debt maturing in the next six weeks. The country will probably be forced to raise taxes and slow public-spending growth. As a result, the economy is likely to slow, unemployment could rise, and some companies will probably not survive. This year so far 7 of the 40 largest 'chaebol' (industrial groups) have become insolvent.

The Korean company Halla Engineering & Heavy Industry Co. says it will cut its 6055-person work force by half.

Wednesday 26 November

In Japan, Tokuyo City Bank collapses.

Thursday 27 November

More than 37,000 South Korean students are enrolled in US colleges and universities, contributing at least $600 million to the US economy. Tourists spend another $2 billion in the US each year. The country is the United

States' fifth-largest export market, buying more than $26 billion worth of American goods in 1996. Across the US commentators are warning that Korea's problems will hit the US hard.

In Japan, Yamaichi Securities' debts are revealed to be worth US$44 billion. It is suggested that if Japan chooses to convert its US treasury bills, American stock and property values would be downgraded substantially.

December 1997

Monday 1 December

Citibank opens a new foreign exchange and treasury dealing room in Singapore. Opening the new facility, Citicorp/Citibank chief executive officer John Reed says that foreign exchange and related business 'accounts for approximately 20–25% of the bank's earnings on a worldwide basis'.

Dr Mahathir says that a bail-out from the IMF 'does not guarantee our economic recovery', adding that 'what is certain is that the bail-out would restrict Malaysia's freedom to design and initiate new ways of stimulating foreign direct investments and the implementation of new economic policies and strategies'.

Analysts say that the financial problems are spreading to Latin America as well as Korea, whose growth is expected to slow sharply. Worldwide growth is now expected to slow to 3.6% next year, still marginally above average world growth over the last ten years. Brazil's currency may crash. The US will suffer if Japan and Latin America stagnate.

The Korean won has fallen by almost 20% this year. Japanese banks are exposed to Korean borrowers, and will probably have to engage in further write-offs. In Hong Kong, short-term interest rates have doubled to 10% in defence of its peg to the dollar.

Wednesday 10 December

Analysts now doubt that the IMF bailout will be enough to maintain the South Korean financial system. The Finance Ministry now says the country's short-term debt is over $100 billion. Five Korean banks have been ordered to close until at least 31 January; they are Nara Banking Corp., Daehan Investment Banking Corp., Shinhan Investment Bank Corp., Hanwha Merchant Bank Corp. and Central Banking Corp.

The state-owned Korea Broadcasting System calls the merchant banks 'the culprits of Korea's economic crisis', saying they are 'digging their own graves' by their use of 'call loans'. The capital market in Korea is almost frozen and there is chaos as the authorities try to stave off collapse.

Thursday 11 December

'Businesses are almost paralyzed', says the chief representative of an American investment bank in Korea. 'They're not out there producing and marketing. They are just trying to get liquidity.' The won is in freefall.

Friday 12 December

The Bank of Japan's (BOJ) chief Yasuo Matsushita admits that the Japanese financial system was severely threatened at one point by the successive collapses of large financial institutions.

Monday 15 December

In Japan, the company bankruptcy rate is sky high. November's debt total was 2.0174 trillion yen, more than 40% more than the total of November 1996.

Tuesday 16 December

The Korean stock market has a record rise of 7.2% on hopes of an accelerated IMF recovery package.

'Everyone in Korea is assuming the worst is over', says a currency trader.

ASEAN leaders begin bilateral meetings with the leaders of China, Japan and South Korea.

Thursday 18 December

Shipyards in Singapore report an upturn in business because of the weakened currency.

Monday 22 December

In Korea President-elect Kim Dae Jung drops his opposition to laying off South Korean workers. He says 'We could go bankrupt even tomorrow'. He publicly renounces a suggestion he made during his presidential campaign to renegotiate the IMF deal.

Moody's downrates several of Korea's top companies including Hyundai Motor Co., LG-Caltex Oil Corp., Yukong (Oil) Ltd, Korea Electric Power, Korea Telecom, Hyundai Semiconductor America Inc., Samsung Electronics Co. and SK Telecom.

In Indonesia, Hyundai Motor cancels a plant after the Indonesian government accepts IMF conditions to lower tariffs on foreign imports and reduce tax breaks for locally produced cars.

Tuesday 23 December

Japanese broker Maruso Securities goes into bankruptcy.

January 1998

Bitter pill needed to cure financial malaise

The Yomiuri Shimbun, 1 January 1998

Thursday 1 January

Richard C. Koo, chief economist at Nomura Research Institute Ltd, is reported as saying that the Japanese economy is in serious trouble: 'On the macroeconomic side, the government embarked on a series of measures for fiscal reconstruction in 1997. Fiscal rehabilitation is similar to a kind of diet that you go on only when you are healthy to begin with. If you are suffering from anaemia, the consequences would be disastrous. Does the Japanese economy really have the strength to go on a diet? By no means. For instance, the economy has not shown any sign of an upturn although the official discount rate has been at a record low of 0.5% for more than two years. In fact, housing starts and sales of new cars, which would usually react favorably to lower interest rates, have been on the decline. In other words, the economy as a whole is fatigued.'

Monday 5 January

The one-month deposit rate for ringgit Asian Currency Units (ACU) dives as low as 2.78%. In November it had been at 6–7%. Holders of fixed-term deposits in ringgit have suffered twice, once from foreign exchange losses and now from lower interest rates.

'Actually the rates are quite good today. We were quoting zero per cent late last month,' said a United Overseas Bank executive.

Following meetings with South Korea's president-elect, George Soros says that the nation's economic crisis is curable and that he is considering a substantial new investment in its troubled markets.

'I saw a clear understanding of the problem and a clear vision of where to go, and that is what makes me interested enough to invest', said Mr Soros, who withdrew virtually all of his investment in South Korea last year but now says he is making plans to 'substantially' increase his investments there.

Tuesday 6 January

Australia's Westpac Banking Corp., is to downsize its staff in Japan. Harold Rosario, the head of Westpac in Japan, says that the bank is transferring back-office support operations to Australia, while maintaining front-office staff levels in Japan, in a plan to centralize administrative support in Australia. The Tokyo branch, which had a staff of 112 in 1990, now consists of 45 people. Rosario says that economic conditions have changed since the Big Bang concept emerged and the measures are not building confidence. 'There was a general belief that Japan would continue to grow 2 percent to 3 percent a year on its own economic activities. However, the market is now showing that economic growth will be zero or maybe negative.'

Wednesday 7 January

Currencies in Indonesia, Thailand, Malaysia and the Philippines tumble to record lows. 'We have seen a major wave of foreign capital flight from Southeast Asia', says Simon Ogus, chief economist for Asia in the Hong

Kong office of SBC Warburg Dillon Read. 'Now we are seeing domestic capital flight. People just don't trust their policymakers in sorting this mess out.'

Tuesday 13 January

Japan debt shock raises pressure on Hashimoto

South China Morning Post, 13 January 1998

Japan's Finance Ministry says that the country's banks are holding 76.7 trillion yen in bad or questionable loans, almost three times the figure previously reported. 'The next question is to what degree [are the bad loans] going to multiply from loans to Asia', says a senior banking analyst. 'God forbid, if they don't tell us the truth again, there's going to be a negative reaction [in the market].'

Wednesday 14 January

Lawrence Summers, deputy US Treasury secretary, rejects claims that the United States is indifferent to Asia's financial crisis and praises Thailand's progress in carrying out economic reforms demanded by the IMF, saying that 'There is no question that this is a critical foreign-policy priority for the US.' He emphasises that Thailand had stuck scrupulously to the conditions of its IMF loan package.

Thursday 15 January

The IMF's managing director Michel Camdessus promises flexibility in its approach to Thailand's wish to change the terms of its $17.2 billion rescue package.

Thai Finance Minister Tarrin Nimmanahaeminda is to travel to Washington for a week from 19 January to meet the IMF and also US Treasury Secretary Robert Rubin, Secretary of State Madeleine Albright and congressional leaders during his trip. His mission is to persuade the IMF that Thailand has met all its reform obligations. There has been strong US Congressional opposition to the IMF's bail-outs for South Korea, Indonesia and Thailand.

Padi Beras Nasional Bhd (Bernas), the custodian of the Malaysian rice industry, has been implementing its government's plan to get Malaysia's Asian trading partners to conduct transactions in their own currencies instead of dollars. The company's managing director says 'We paid for a shipment of 20,000 tonnes of rice from Thailand this month in ringgit while another shipment of 50,000 tonnes from Pakistan, scheduled to arrive early next month, will be paid in rupees'.

Dr Supachai Panitchpakdi, Deputy Prime Minister of Thailand, says that there is a total lack of confidence among the Asian countries arising from the mismanagement of macroeconomic policies. The Thai government, he says, should have warned trade and industry when to slowdown for consolidation of growth, when to maintain the pace and so forth. He gives the example of steel – when steel supply would be redundant in many countries, many steel projects were allowed to start. Speaking at the Partnership Summit '98 organised by the Confederation of Indian Industry (CII), Dr Supachai says that the financial turmoil is a blessing in disguise since it 'forced us to look at governance and look at liberalisation in full-fledged terms and to work more closely in the ASEAN region, where the hardworking countries needed to maintain growth and pace.'

Monday 19 January

The former deputy managing director of the Monetary Authority of Singapore Koh Beng Seng is to become a part-time adviser to the IMF in Thailand to help monitor reforms. Observers in Asia say he is an excellent choice and is reputed to have been responsible for Singapore's robust approach to the regulation of its financial sector.

Bankruptcies break records, worst yet to come

Asahi Shimbun, 20 January 1998.

Tuesday 20 January

In Japan, bankruptcy liabilities reach a record high of 14.02 trillion yen in 1997 and are expected to grow worse in the coming months. 16,365 corporations, each with debts of 10 million yen or more, failed between January and December.

Japanese analysts say they expect the bankruptcy rate to worsen.

Wednesday 21 January

On a visit to Thailand, Singapore Senior Minister Lee Kuan Yew says that the economic crisis in Thailand must be resolved quickly – 'Thailand is the first country to be in the (IMF) programme. If it can implement it and show the rest of the world that this is the right way to go ... then confidence in the markets will improve, and the survival of these countries will be a lot clearer in everyone's mind.'

Thursday 22 January

US–ASEAN Business Council president Ernest Bower says that US companies will be supportive of an ASEAN proposal to use local currencies for intra-ASEAN commercial transactions.

Friday 23 January

A row erupts in Japan over whether Yamaichi Securities Co. was within its rights to unilaterally decide to close. The Asahi Shimbun reports Michio Sato, former chief prosecutor in Sapporo and now an Upper House member in the Japanese parliament, as saying, 'It is clearly a violation of the Commercial Law to decide to close a company without first consulting with its shareholders. The law stipulates that a corporate dissolution and even a business transfer requires the approval of at least two-thirds of the total quorum at a shareholders meeting. The decision ignored (Yamaichi) shareholders. It is as undemocratic as it is authoritarian.'

Monday 26 January

In Malaysia, Entrepreneur Development Minister Datuk Mustapa Mohamed says that the depreciation of the ringgit will enable the Mara agency to 'sponsor 10 students to pursue tertiary education locally rather than only one to study overseas'. Mara will completely cease sponsoring students for overseas education by the year 2000.

In the currency markets, trading in Asian currencies is slow but steady as the Lunar New Year and Moslem Eid al-Fitr holidays approach. The US dollar is weak owing to the latest sex scandal involving President Clinton, giving the Asian currencies a welcome respite.

The Bank of Thailand takes over the troubled Bangkok Metropolitan Bank.

Tuesday 27 January

The IMF agrees to changes in the conditions of the $17.2 billion rescue package for Thailand.

A statement from the Thai government says 'The IMF has agreed that there will be a change in Thailand's economic package to ensure the conditions are more in line with the economic situation, which has changed, and the regional economic situation', asserting that the country's economic slump is damaging government revenue and having social consequences. Details of the changes are still to be negotiated.

Analysts predict an eventual end to family-run banking businesses in Thailand.

Bank Indonesia intervenes in the currency markets to support the rupiah. 'The central bank sold a limited amount of dollars through state banks, and it proved to be effective in arresting the rupiah's fall', says a dealer. 'The intervention was effective because most players were reluctant to take positions for fear of a possible strengthening rupiah on news that Japan will help Indonesia handle its financial crisis.'

Latest

Wednesday 11 March

The credit squeeze imposed by Japan's banks is starting to hit smaller Japanese companies hard. They are facing their most serious cash flow problems in 20 years according to government-linked lending agency, Shoko Chukin.

China reports that industrial output growth in the first two months of the year has slowed to 8% (compared to 10.4% in the corresponding period of 1997).

Suharto presidency nodded through

Financial Times (London), 11 March 1998

Part 2

The End of the Miracle?

Chapter 1

Enter the IMF

When the troubled Asian countries realised the extent of their difficulties, it was plain that they needed loans from elsewhere; countries which were in a position to lend, however, were insisting on IMF involvement in any bail-out.

As we have seen, the 'contagion' began in Thailand, whose competitiveness had clearly been eroding, partly because of the baht peg to the dollar, and partly because it had been slower than its neighbours in developing its infrastructure. A weak banking sector, increasing short-term foreign debt and a gross property boom based on that debt were just a few of the signals that the country was heading for trouble. The International Monetary Fund (IMF) had been warning the country of these problems, but too little remedial action had been taken.

IMF loans hurt; they force governments to close down favoured institutions if they are insolvent and to impose unpopular restrictions on their countries' economies. These drastic actions are often seen as unfair, but countries are, in financial terms, the same as individuals and companies – if they spend far more than they earn they eventually run out of credit and must face unpleasantness:

- their currency will buy less abroad
- they must import less
- they must ruthlessly reform their banking system and close insolvent institutions
- they must reduce government spending.

Under the IMF system, the country itself chooses its reform programme, but has to satisfy the IMF – representing the majority will of its member states – that the reforms will be enough to put the country back on a sound footing.

The troubled Asian countries accept that they do not have enough specialist personnel in central banking and public finance, so the IMF provides advisers and training facilities to help with the complex task of reform as it has done with many other countries over the years.

The public in the Asian countries were understandably confused at these developments. Jet Magsaysay, of *World Executive Digest* in the Philippines, describes the popular reaction as follows:

> *'The financial industry is so esoteric that very few people outside it really understand it. They will tend to be confused rather than enlightened by any political pronouncements about currency speculation and so forth. To a certain extent I think that the real problem in Asia is that people don't understand what terms such as currency speculation mean in the first place – even a large percentage of the business world does not. The net result is that people just don't know what to think about it all.'*

This public confusion is normal – it invariably occurs when there is a shock to a country's economy. Politicians then face the difficult task of dealing with legitimate public concern while implementing tough economic measures. Thus it is no coincidence that there have been changes of government in Thailand and Korea.

The IMF in Asia

No-one in a country which has to borrow from the IMF enjoys the experience, as UK citizens who remember the 1977 bail-out can attest, so it is not surprising that the populations of the Asian countries who are now the recipients of IMF-sponsored loan packages are confused and suspicious. IMF loans come with unpalatable conditions attached – for example, the borrowing country cannot:

- Use the IMF loan to prevent non-financial institutions from going bankrupt. Thus it cannot, for example, bolster a manufacturer which is in trouble.
- Use the IMF loan to save a financial institution which is insolvent.
- Compensate shareholders of financial institutions which go bankrupt or suffer heavy losses.
- Compensate people such as bank customers for losses without the IMF's agreement.

Important

At the time of writing, information was available on the IMF's deals with Thailand, Indonesia and Korea; the precise details could change week by week as efforts to defuse the crisis continue.

Thailand

- 58 of 91 finance firms have been suspended and 56 will be liquidated.
- Shareholders' equity and subordinated debt in unviable finance companies will be written down to cover losses.
- In 16 of the suspended finance companies, depositors will receive interest-bearing 'non-negotiable instruments' (in effect IOUs that cannot be borrowed against), which specify a certain date for payment of between 6 and 60 months. The other suspending companies will suffer slightly less onerous strictures.
- All other local finance companies and banks will pay their depositors in baht on demand.
- All the viable financial institutions must apply stricter lending rules and increase their own capital.

- Once the banking system is made sound, guarantees for depositors and others will be backed by a self-financed deposit insurance scheme, with limited coverage of deposits.

Thailand is receiving $17.2 billion from the package, supplied by:

	$ billion
IMF	4
World Bank	1.5
Asian Development Bank	1.2
Japan	4
Australia	1
China	1
Hong Kong	1
Malaysia	1
Singapore	1
Indonesia	0.5
South Korea	0.5

South Korea

- Nearly half of South Korea's investment banks (14 of 30) have been suspended. Any that are not recapitalised and shown to be viable within a fixed period will be closed down.
- The other investment banks must produce plans to show how their situation will be made sound and if the authorities do not accept the plans or they are not implemented, the banks will be closed.
- Two troubled commercial banks must merge with sound banks (foreign or local) within a set period. At present the government controls them and is providing temporary money to support them.
- The South Korean government has fully guaranteed all deposit claims of local residents. This scheme will be fully funded by the government but will be replaced by a scheme limited to small depositors and financed by covered institutions in the year 2000.

- If financial institutions are closed, payments will only be made to in-sured creditors and the losses will be borne by the shareholders and uninsured creditors.

South Korea's central bank, the Bank of Korea, is supported by government and government guaranteed securities. The IMF-sponsored package of $57 billion is made up of:

	$ billion
IMF	21
World Bank	10
Asian Development Bank	4
A group of industrial countries	22

Australia, Belgium, Canada, France, Germany, Italy, Japan, the Netherlands, Sweden, Switzerland, the United Kingdom, and the United States have told the IMF that they will provide further support if necessary.

Indonesia

- The government has announced that it will withdraw tax breaks and monopoly rights in key sectors dominated by businesses run by President Suharto's family and close associates, such as the tax breaks on the Timor national car project, run by Suharto's son 'Tommy' Hutomo Mandala Putra.
- 16 banks have been closed. Their shareholders will not be compensated and the banks' debts will not be repaid by the government except for small deposit-making customers who will get up to 20 million rupees each per bank. The scheme will be paid for by the government and administered by the Bank of Indonesia.
- Other viable banks must produce rehabilitation plans which must be approved by the central bank or else they must go into receivership.

- Bank Indonesia will improve its 'lender of last resort' function, providing loans to troubled banks under stringent conditions.
- State banks will be downsized, privatised and subject to international auditing standards. Development banks in the different regions will be closed if not made viable within a year. The Indonesian government will not guarantee the debts of any company not in the finance sector.

The Indonesian package totals $35 billion, made up of:

	$ billion
IMF	10
World Bank	4.5
Asian Development Bank	3.5
Japan	5
Singapore	5
Australia	1
Malaysia	1
China	1
Hong Kong(China)	1
USA	3

What is the IMF?

The majority of people across the world are understandably mystified by this organisation and suspicion of its motives abound. The IMF is not an aid organisation, nor is it the world's central bank. It is an organisation controlled by its 182 member countries and is intended to assist these countries in their efforts to keep the system of buying and selling one another's currencies stable. The IMF lends money to members having trouble meeting financial obligations to other members on condition that they implement economic reforms. It has no direct political power – it can, and often does, advise member countries not to spend their money foolishly, but it cannot in normal circumstances force a member country to change its policies.

Because money payments between states are so important to world economic stability, the IMF's members have given it the power to demand the disclosure of financial information from any one of their number. The organisation acts as monitor of foreign currency payments across the world, providing a vital source of information to its members. Without a stable system of currency exchange, world trade cannot flourish and grow.

As World War II drew to a close, the Allied nations and their supporters met in the US at Bretton Woods in New Hampshire to plan an international monetary system for the post-war era. They created the International Monetary Fund and the World Bank, and set up a system which was intended to provide stability to exchange rates. Since the victorious USA had become by far the most powerful country in the world, the system was tied to the US dollar at $33 to an ounce of gold. All other currencies were defined in terms of dollars. If a country wanted to change its rate of exchange against the dollar, it had to make a formal announcement that it was revaluing, or devaluing, its currency. In 1949, 28 countries devalued their currencies.

As world trade mushroomed after World War II and the economic balance between countries began to change, vast funds grew up which were highly mobile and could be switched from one country to another without the permission of governments. The demand for gold was high, and the official price of $33 to an ounce was undermined by the creation of secondary markets where gold was traded at much higher prices. As its economic strength diminished, the USA decided unilaterally to abandon the Bretton Woods system when, in 1971, it suspended the right to convert dollars for gold at $33 to the ounce, and devalued the dollar.

The floating exchange rate system

Bretton Woods was supplanted by the floating exchange rate system in which currencies are not formally linked to any other, or to gold. The rate at which you can exchange one currency for another is simply the best rate that someone will give you, so exchange rates are highly volatile (this is why they are called 'floating').

During the oil crises of 1973 and 1979, for example, when OPEC dramatically increased the price of oil, the floating system helped to minimise the chaos, as the strain was taken by an adjustment in exchange rates (the OPEC countries' currencies suddenly became much more valuable), rather than by curtailing real economic activity, as would have happened if the Bretton Woods system had still been operating.

The floating exchange rate system has disadvantages and there are many examples today of currencies that are 'pegged' to others. Most of the South East Asian countries pegged their currencies to the US dollar, with the encouragement of overseas investors and money managers. The motive was to attract more foreign capital into their countries.

The peg works as a kind of guarantee for foreign investors that the local currencies – usually thought of as 'soft' currencies – will not fluctuate wildly. Thus pegs reduce the short-term risk for overseas investors. Prior to the crisis the general consensus in the investment world was that currency pegs were a good thing both for Asia and for foreign investors. Technically, the pegs were 'dirty floats', which means that the local currency was allowed to fluctuate freely against the dollar within a very narrow range.

As we will see in the next chapter, currency pegging is only a limited form of guarantee. If there is a crisis, then the authorities may be forced to allow their currencies to float freely, which effectively means that there will be a sudden and serious devaluation. This is exactly what did happen in Thailand and Indonesia.

How the IMF has grown

During the Great Depression of the 1930s, it was clear that something like the IMF was needed to prevent the devastation and suffering caused by the freeze in international trade – between 1929 and 1932 prices of goods fell by 48% worldwide, and the value of international trade fell by 63%. The financial markets were in chaos and there was a general distrust of paper money which led to nations hoarding gold, restricting currency exchange (thus damaging their trade with other countries even further) and artificially devaluing their own currencies in attempts to make their own exports seem cheaper abroad. This last activity, called 'competitive devaluation', merely led to rival nations following suit and a general confusion about the 'true' value of objects.

By the end of World War II, caused at least in part by the Depression which preceded it, capitalist countries everywhere were very ready for a firm solution to the problems of world trade. The IMF began operations in Washington, DC in May 1946. It then had 39 members.

Any country that has control over its own foreign policy can become a member of the IMF if it wishes; today, the former communist states of Eastern Europe and the USSR are all members. If a country wishes to leave the IMF it may do so – Indonesia and Poland, for instance, left the IMF, only to rejoin later. The only country to have left the IMF that has not rejoined is Cuba.

Who controls the IMF?

When a country joins, it agrees to pay the IMF sums of money called its 'quota subscription'. This money is used in several ways:

- It forms a fund that the IMF can use to lend to members in financial difficulty.
- It is used to calculate how much a member can draw from the IMF – the more it pays in, the more it can borrow.
- The amount of the quota is used to calculate the voting power of the member state.

When a country joins, the IMF sets the amount of the quota. As you might expect, rich countries pay higher quotas than poor ones. The amount of the quota is reviewed periodically. The US is the largest contributor and has about 18% of the total vote – thus it does not have a 'majority shareholding' in the organisation, although its voice is powerful.

To emphasise the point, the IMF does not tell its members what to do – its members decide on the IMF's policies. The IMF's Executive Board rarely makes its decisions on the basis of formal voting, however, but relies on the formation of consensus among its members to reduce confrontation on sensitive issues and promote agreement on decisions.

About 2200 people work for the IMF. Its managing director is traditionally not a US national. The staff come from over 100 countries and are mainly economists; most of them work at the HQ in Washington, DC.

The IMF's 'surveillance'

The IMF is mandated to 'exercise firm surveillance' over each of its members' exchange rate policies, involving the assessment of their economic policies. This is done systematically, with the IMF conducting annual consultations with most members to review their economies and see how changes could affect other members; social issues are examined among other matters.

Globalisation has made the IMF far more concerned with issues relating to the financial sector in the short to medium term. It has been recognised for several years that information technology and globalisation have increased the potential volatility of economies. Members are now asked to provide monthly data although it is thought that not all do so.

It is now generally thought that fiscal 'transparency' – in other words, keeping fewer secrets – is important to keep the world's economy stable. Many member countries are now trying to be more open about their economic policies than hitherto, and the IMF itself has also become more open, publishing large amounts of information that is not restricted.

The General Arrangements to Borrow (GAB)

The GAB is a system which allows the IMF to borrow extra money from 11 wealthy members; this allows it to assist member states who are in trouble even if its own funds are low. This has been done nine times so far, most recently in 1977 when the IMF lent to the UK and Italy, and in 1978 when it lent to the US. If the GAB fails, the IMF is allowed to take short-term loans from any source it wishes. At present, it has no debt.

Conclusion

The IMF exists in order to keep international currency exchange stable. Once Korea, Thailand and Indonesia recover, the stringent IMF conditions will no longer apply – it will once again become easier to borrow money. Hopefully, the countries' banking systems will emerge in a more robust form, able to withstand any future shocks. How long this process will take, and what effects it will have on the way that Asians do business, cannot yet be known.

Chapter 2

Those Wicked Speculators

The Asian financial crisis started in the currency markets and many people – including some politicians, notably Malaysia's Dr Mahathir – appear to blame international speculation for their countries' problems. From the point of view of economists, however, this cannot be a correct analysis. Let's take the example of Thailand, where the trouble began.

Thailand has a high personal savings rate and had been growing fast – two factors one might regard as healthy – but its banking system was weak. Foreign investors saw this weakness and were worried that it would adversely affect Thailand's property and stock markets. They feared that if things went wrong they would not be able to get their money back from local banks and financial institutions that became insolvent. The government's budget had had a surplus in the run-up to the crisis, but its current account was in the red at about 8% of the nation's total GDP. Like a fast-growing company, Thailand was getting into short-term debt even though it was technically 'making profits' – too much money was being borrowed from foreign sources.

So why didn't foreign investors pull out earlier? It appears that the baht's peg to the dollar and the government's reassurances that local banks would not be allowed to fail were sufficiently convincing for foreign investors to be unable to resist the high interest rates that Thai banks were paying even though there had been warnings – instances of speculation against the baht occurred in 1996 and at the very beginning of 1997.

The Thai government had not been unresponsive; it had tightened its monetary policy and fiscal policy and took action on many fronts in accordance with the advice of the best economic experts. Two apparent mistakes were made:

1 Hanging on to a narrow band for its exchange rate for too long. This encouraged more foreign money into the country since there seemed to be no danger of a sharp drop in the baht's value.
2 Allowing offshore financial institutions to borrow foreign money and then lending it too freely to local Thais. The government allowed banks to hide the true extent of their lending on Thai real estate and did not force them to reveal their bad debts.

With so much money pouring into the country, Thai banks began to lend more and more dangerously, even running out of sufficiently qualified staff to make the lending decisions.

When foreign money suddenly started to leave and the baht's peg was dropped, Thai banks found themselves without any insurance against the possibility of a devaluation of the baht – they had been too confident in the currency peg. Likewise, Thai businesses and individuals had happily borrowed in foreign currencies without thought of the risk, and they were now faced with hugely increased repayment costs because the baht was worth less in terms of the currencies they had borrowed.

This is where the currency speculators come in. Seeing that the baht was likely to remain weak, they were able to conduct complex deals in the international currency markets which had the effect of forcing the baht down even further, leading to chaos and bankruptcies within the country. The IMF then had to step in to prevent Thailand from total financial collapse and assist it in 'adjusting' its economy to regain soundness.

As we have seen, certain Asian politicians' criticisms of currency speculators were vociferous. Can Dr Mahathir's *ad hominem* attacks on George

Soros be justified? Soros is, after all, just one of many specialists controlling vast funds of cash which are used to trade for profit in the high risk currency markets.

George Soros is a well-known figure and is easy to blame for devaluations since his Quantum Fund's notoriously high profits from the British pound when it left the ERM on 'Black Wednesday' in 1992. The activities of currency traders are generally obscure, incidentally – it is rarely the case that the full details of their trades become public knowledge. It is believed, however, that in 1996 Soros' trading cost the Bank of Thailand at least $4 billion, as the BOT rallied support for regional central banks to fend off Soros' attack on the baht. Typically, Soros' only comment was ' I don't want to comment on the baht because we've been attacked by the Thai government and there have been some exaggerated rumours.'

Currency speculators do not rule the world; they are best seen as a force providing liquidity in the world's currency markets and a 'reality check' for the central banks who supervise their countries' exchange rates. They will always 'attack' a currency where they perceive weakness, since that is how they make large profits. If they are wrong, they lose money; there is no evident political motive behind their actions. In contrast to Dr Mahathir, Indonesia's President Soeharto said in parliament that if speculators attacked a currency they were merely going about a natural business which would sort out the weak from the strong – if the speculators succeed and an economy stumbles, then this is the responsibility of the country itself.

Yet it is not only in South East Asia that speculators were initially blamed for the crisis. Korea, too, was severely critical of them. Professor Jae Ho Park of Seoul University describes the mood late last year: 'We were angry, but mainly angry at ourselves. How could we have allowed this to happen to us? And we had been encouraged to liberalise our economy – it was as if the rules of boxing were suddenly changed so that heavyweights could fight flyweights. In a match like that, of course the flyweight is going to get killed.'

The floating exchange rate system discussed in Chapter 1 does not operate in its pure form in Asia, which mostly operates currency pegging (usually to the US dollar, controlled by a monetary authority (generally a central bank). Managing a country's exchange rate allows the appreciation or depreciation of a currency to happen in a more orderly way, in theory, at least. This has been the case in Singapore, but South Korea, which also operates a managed float, has not avoided chaos.

The supply and demand for money

Arguably a major factor in the currency crisis in South East Asia has been competition from China and Japan. In global markets for low value-added goods, such as textiles, China is pushing out South East Asia because it can produce those goods more cheaply. With high value-added goods, such as cars, the depreciation of the yen has made Japanese products more competitive. This competitive squeeze at both ends has been a potent force in bringing about a need for South East Asia to adjust, but the currency pegging has meant that the necessary devaluations have been sharp and painful.

Ultimately, money is governed by supply and demand. Central banks control how much of their country's money is in circulation but the purchasing power of that money is subject to market forces. The real demand for money fluctuates and cannot be forecast exactly; market forces adjust the real supply of money to the real demand.

With a floating exchange rate, if the real supply of money exceeds the real demand, the exchange rate depreciates, thus decreasing the purchasing power of the currency. If the real supply is less than the real demand, the exchange rate appreciates, increasing the purchasing power of the currency.

In a fixed-rate system it is the amount of money in circulation rather than the exchange rate that adjusts. If the real supply of money exceeds the real demand, losses of foreign reserves cause the central bank to reduce the amount of money in circulation. If the opposite happens the central bank can increase the amount of money in circulation.

The minutiae of the work of central banks are arcane but the essential points to understand are:

- They act as the 'lender of last resort' to other banks in their country. This gives stability to the local banking system and a limited guarantee that bank depositors will not lose all their money in a collapse. As we have seen, while small depositors have received some protection from IMF bail-outs, shareholders of insolvent banks, and many creditors, have suffered major losses.
- They oversee the operations of local banks. Arguably, the central banks of countries such as Thailand have failed in this regard by being too lax.
- They control the amount of credit that local banks are giving customers – once again a point of weakness in the affected countries.
- They control the issue and circulation of coins and notes.
- They administer government-issued bonds.
- They are their own government's banker in the same way as local banks act for their customers.

One of the short-term actions that a central bank can take is to buy large amounts of its own currency in the world's foreign exchange (forex) markets to make it stronger against other currencies, or to sell it in order to make it weaker. Ultimately, market forces will decide on exchange rates, but for a certain period central banks can 'artificially' influence exchange rates by this means. A central bank may try to make its exports more competitive by keeping its currency weaker – as Japan and the UK have attempted to do in the recent past. In the case of the Asian countries in crisis, the central banks attempted to keep the value of their currencies high against other currencies.

How forex markets work

To grasp how forex works, imagine that you have a business. If you are importing from abroad, say, you will normally pay for the goods in the currency of the country of origin, so, if you are a Thai importer, you'll pay a German supplier in marks, a US supplier in dollars and so on. Both the private and the public sectors do this. In order to pay your supplier in his currency, you need to exchange your currency. This is done through banks as a service, but ultimately the foreign currency is purchased on the foreign exchange market.

The foreign exchange market is international, and consists of banks, brokers and others buying and selling currencies from most of the countries in the world. Often exchange rates change several times a minute, so high-tech communications are vital. The main centres for foreign exchange trading are New York, London, Tokyo, Zurich and Frankfurt, which turn over hundreds of billions of dollars a day. Thus, although most other countries, including Malaysia, Hong Kong and Singapore, have their own foreign exchange markets, much of their countries' currencies are traded in the main centres abroad, out of control of the local authorities. This is an important point – when a currency is attacked, most of the action does not occur within the country itself.

In the forex markets, the US dollar is king. Known as a 'vehicle currency', it is the most frequently traded and is normally used for doing business in commodities such as coffee, gold and oil. In the free market system, businesses act out of self-interest – they will use certain currencies because it is the cheapest or most profitable way to complete transactions. Businesses often find that it is cheaper, say, to buy dollars and then convert them to another foreign currency than to buy that currency directly with their own.

Currency futures

As well as simply providing the means to exchange currencies at will (the 'spot' exchange rate) the forex markets enable bargains to be struck and settled at a future date. This is an essential part of their function because business needs stability.

Suppose a German company purchases from an Indonesian supplier goods which are to be paid for in three months' time. If it waits until the due date before exchanging its currency, the exchange rate may have changed and the cost, in Deutschmark terms, may be higher or lower. This gives the company extra exchange rate risk which it may not want, in which case it can arrange ahead of time to purchase the Indonesian currency at an agreed 'forward' rate. The transaction will still occur on the same date as before, but the company is more interested in being sure what its liability will be in three months' time than in speculating, so no sleep is lost over the gamble. It has protected itself against any unpleasant surprises by making a 'forward contract'. This is known as 'hedging'.

Currency arbitrage

Financial institutions who operate in the forex markets are able to make profits from 'arbitrage' when the exchange rates for two given currencies are slightly different in different forex markets. If, for instance, the dollar/yen rate is momentarily different in Frankfurt and London, the currency trader can purchase it in one market and sell it instantaneously in the other for a tiny profit. Such a profit is, however, virtually risk free. Arbitrageurs are usually banks – the activity requires a heavy investment in technology and the ability to monitor and trade across the world's forex markets at all times. Transactions are usually huge, so even if the profit is only a fraction of 1%, it still represents a large sum of money. Banks have specialist departments that search for arbitrage opportunities across a wide range of financial instruments, an activity which has become increasingly sophisticated and arcane since the introduction of information technology.

Currency speculation

Speculation differs from arbitrage in that real risks are taken – you are trying to make money by predicting future rates of exchange rather than looking for momentary mismatches between exchange rates as arbitrageurs do. Once again, very large sums of money are involved, meaning that most speculation is done by financial institutions. The individuals who actually conduct the trades live very aggressive, high-stressed lives – the risks are high – and are under no illusions about their task, which is purely and simply to make money. If a country's currency appears vulnerable, speculators will 'attack' by selling that currency on the forex markets in the main financial centres in the hope of driving the price down still further, using complex patterns of spot and forward trading combined with other derivatives.

No-one can predict the future with great accuracy, and it is notoriously difficult to predict exchange rates. Speculators are the most 'short-termist' of all financial players – they are principally interested in what is going to happen next, rather than in what will happen in five or ten years' time.

Nevertheless, they do try to predict the future of currencies by considering:

- Inflation. Countries with high inflation relative to other countries find that the prices of the goods and services that they export rise also. This leads to fewer customers for their goods, a higher amount of imports, consequent trading losses and a weakening currency.
- Monthly and quarterly trade figures. These tend to be far less reliable than the annual balance of payment accounts, which are not very reliable either. Nevertheless, the foreign exchange market grasps eagerly for such interim figures as they are published, in the hope of finding clues about the future.
- Flows of capital. If, for example, a country is trading at a loss but is enjoying a large amount of investment from abroad, its currency may not weaken as it otherwise would.

- Interest rates. A country which offers a higher rate of interest than others do will often attract money from abroad in the short term. However, if investors believe that the currency is likely to become worth less, they will switch their money to a safer currency.
- Investment abroad. Countries whose companies are purchasing or setting up businesses overseas are generally thought to have currencies which will get stronger for a decade or more, since it will take that length of time for the companies to make their profits.
- Money flowing into a country's stock markets. This is usually a sign that the currency will be strong, at least for three years or so.
- Productivity. A country with a high rate of productivity and economic growth is often thought to have a strengthening currency. If growth seems to be slowing – as in Asia – then the currency may weaken.
- Savings. Populations who spend everything they earn make their currencies weaker by increasing trading losses. It is notable that economically strong countries, such as Japan, have a high rate of saving per head of population.
- Confidence in policies. Investors from outside a country will look at its political situation to assess the risks of investing there. Not many people will buy bonds, for example, from a government which looks as if it is collapsing.
- Bull and bear markets. As with shares, if investors think that a currency is increasing or decreasing, they will invest accordingly, creating a self-fulfilling prophecy in the short term.
- Singular events. Wars, commodity price hikes and other one-off occurrences will have short-term effects on exchange rates.

The Asian crisis is interesting because many of these considerations were positive – a high rate of private savings and productivity and a generally stable political environment, for instance. This strongly suggests that the currencies will not spiral downwards indefinitely – as Asia adjusts its economies to the shock, its currencies seem likely to stabilise and gradually improve.

Conclusion

Devaluation of a country's currency is rarely popular amongst its inhabitants but is an occasional fact of life. Countries that borrow to finance their growth need to take care not to assume that the foreign money will always pour in without a hiccup; such inflows can be halted at any time in a free market. Currently there are proposals for a regional Asian fund, paid for by member countries, which would be used to help support any member's central bank when it wished to intervene in the forex markets; the jury is out on this idea, but critics say that this could compound future problems by making all the Asian countries at risk if one member made a mistake.

Chapter 3

Sustainable Development?

Although the vast amount of investment in the region's infrastructure and manufacturing base is not generally thought to be a direct cause of the current crisis, questions have been raised about whether many projects are really necessary. Overcapacity is already a serious problem in much of the electronics industry and is predicted to become one in the manufacture of silicon chips. Furthermore, the long-term consequences of overdevelopment should be examined; environmental issues, in particular, are likely to become increasingly important considerations and, since the Rio Earth Summit of 1992, are no longer thought of as marginal to the business of economic development.

Before considering the problems that Asia's success has brought, we should remind ourselves of what it has achieved:

- A dramatic reduction in poverty – in a single lifetime, millions of Asians have escaped destitution. Incomes in South Korea, for instance, have quadrupled in the last 20 years.
- Five Asian countries are among the 12 largest economies in the world; they are China, Japan, India, Indonesia and South Korea. World-class Asian companies include Toyota, Samsung, Acer, Hong Kong Bank and Singapore Airlines.
- A new Asian middle class has arisen to become an important market in global terms and trade barriers are coming down. For instance, Samsung defines 'middle class' as those people who own or can afford a washing machine, a refrigerator, a television, a microwave oven and a VCR. By this definition the vast majority of South Koreans are middle class.

- Better nutrition across the region is resulting in taller, healthier people – in Japan, for instance, teenagers are estimated to be around 8% taller than they were 20 years ago.
- Tertiary education has mushroomed. In Hong Kong, for example, the number of undergraduates has increased by more than 400% since 1975.
- The introduction of information technology and the new media. Since 1990, satellite TV has become widely available in the region. China has had a 3000% increase in telephone calls abroad since the mid-1980s. Fibre-optic cables are being laid widely in the region.
- A new willingness amongst Asian states to co-operate. When ASEAN began in the mid-1970s, the communist countries of Indo-China called it a tool of American imperialism. Now Vietnam and China are members and Cambodia, Laos and Myanmar have observer status
- In 1970, Asia had only eight cities with more than five million inhabitants. Now there are over 30.
- There have been massive increases in the number of roads, railways and electricity production across the region.

Sustainable development

In 1972, the United Nations Conference on the Human Environment, held at Stockholm, was the first major discussion of environmental issues at the international level. It was soon plain that while the developed countries were seriously concerned about how economic development and industrial pollution were threatening the natural environment, the developing countries felt that the alleviation of poverty was such a pressing need that economic growth should continue as quickly as possible, regardless of the effects on the environment.

In 1987 the Brundtland Report introduced the notion of 'sustainable development', which has gone some way to resolve the conflicting views. 'Sustainable development' is the idea that governments should integrate their economic, social and environmental policies to allow economic growth which can continue in the long term – the argument being that long-term growth is dependent on the maintenance of the natural environment and that this maintenance can only be paid for by such growth.

By 1992, these ideas were becoming generally accepted and the United Nations Conference on Environment and Development, better known as the 'Earth Summit', was held in Rio de Janeiro. The focus now was on how to implement plans, rather than to argue about the issues, as had been the case in Stockholm. An action plan was produced, 'Agenda 21', which affirmed the main recommendation of the Brundtland Report.

Like other developing countries, Asian nations generally agree with the principle of sustainable development. The problem is the cost. Asia seeks to acquire the affluence that the rich West already has, and cannot afford to spend all its money on environmental protection. One source of revenue that could eventually provide the solution is the nascent 'eco-tourism' industry.

There is no doubt that Asia is already suffering from some of the effects of its rapid growth; here are a few examples:

- China is now believed to be the world's most polluted country. Certain Chinese cities are invisible from space because of the clouds of pollution hovering over them.
- Thailand and the Philippines have experienced catastrophic deforestation. In the Philippines, for instance, there is less than one million hectares of original forest left – in the 1960s there were 15 million hectares.
- In Thailand's capital Bangkok there is virtually no treatment of sewage. The raw effluent produced by six million inhabitants pours into the city's open Chao Phraya river. Lead levels in Bangkok's children are dangerously high.

The haze

As euphemisms go, the 'haze' is a beauty. The 1997 forest fires of South East Asia are a man-made catastrophe which, while only the fifth largest of what have been almost annual events during the last 20 years, attracted worldwide attention as a vast pall of smoke drifted across South East Asia for months, covering Singapore and Malaysia and reaching parts of Thailand and the Philippines.

The scale of the devastation is hard to comprehend. The official Indonesian estimate is that 265,000 hectares (655,000 acres) of forests in the country burned down in 1997. With over 100 million hectares of forests in Indonesia, this represents the destruction of around 0.25% of all the forests within a matter of months. Other estimates of the destruction, however, are as high as two million hectares lost.

In October 1997, the Indonesian government revoked the logging licences of 29 companies (some of them state-owned) for not reporting their alleged fire-starting activities. The sanctioned companies include some owned by Indonesia's wealthiest tycoons, such as Bob Hasan, President Soeharto's golf partner. Prosecutions are unlikely and there is a press embargo on reporting on the timber companies' role in the fires. A sizeable number of logging firms are operating without licences. Several fires in Kalimantan are located in a million-hectare area of marshland that President Soeharto personally designated to be cleared for agricultural use.

President Soeharto took the remarkable step of apologising to neighbouring countries for the haze, which has caused over 1000 deaths in the region. Human casualties from the fires included:

- 234 passengers killed in an Indonesian aeroplane crash on Sumatra due to poor visibility
- 29 dead when a supertanker collided with a merchant vessel in the Strait of Malacca
- tens of thousands receiving treatment for lung infections, asthma and other haze-related complaints.

The fires are expected to return next year because of the unusually prolonged dry season caused by the 'El Niño' effect. As of February, there were still fires burning on Borneo, despite vigorous efforts to put them out on the part of Indonesia and Malaysia.

The Bakun dam

An example of the high aspirations of development in Asia is the controversial Bakun Dam hydroelectric project, currently under construction in the Malaysian state of Sarawak on the island of Borneo, which has gone through many mutations since it was first mooted over ten years ago. At its most ambitious, the dam was to have provided electricity for the whole island of Borneo – including the independent country of Brunei and the Indonesian state of Kalimantan – and also to Singapore, peninsular Malaysia and possibly the Philippines.

The 200 metre high rockfill dam was planned to have a maximum output of 2400 megawatts of which only a small proportion was intended for Sarawak itself. The dam is to be half a mile (c. 800 metres) wide, blocking a flooded area covering some 300 square miles (c. 770 square kilometres) – about the size of New York. To conduct electricity to peninsular Malaysia, the world's longest underwater cable link was proposed, running 670 kilometres under the South China Sea.

Although it is a private project being built by the Malaysian company Ekran Berhad, there is strong government involvement in its financing following alleged difficulties for Ekran in raising money internationally.

Objections to the project have centred around three main points – the effects on between 5000 and 10,000 indigenous people who will lose their lands under the waters of the dam, the destruction of a large area of virgin rainforest, and disagreements over whether Malaysia really 'needs' the electricity. Opposition to the dam's construction has been energetic. In 1990 the project was cancelled but in 1993 it was resurrected. In early 1996 three indigenous residents of the affected area took Ekran and the government to court and in June the High Court ruled in their favour, declaring that the government had failed to comply with its own environmental laws when it approved the project. This ruling was later overturned on appeal.

During the summer of 1997 it appeared that the project might once again be halted, but as Malaysia has already spent $100 million on Bakun, it clearly has to be finished in some form. The most recent plans are to build a 1200-megawatt dam, half the original capacity, which is expected to begin operating in 2006, serving Borneo alone. This scaled-down version appears to be a reasonable compromise, but it remains to be seen whether the project will, in hindsight, seem a necessary part of the area's infrastructure or an overambitious mistake.

Signs of overcapacity

It has been clear for some time that Asia will not continue to grow simply by continuing to rely on low-cost manufacturing. Nor will Western corporations be able to generate profits indefinitely by supplying Asia's strong demand for power generation, car manufacturing and telecommunications.

Much of the endeavour in recent years has been devoted to following Japan's lead in moving up from the lower end of manufacturing to 'high value-added' industries such as car making and petrochemicals. Now there is a serious danger of overcapacity in these sectors and in consumer electronics and silicon chip manufacture as well. In 1997, for instance, a surplus of petrochemicals in the world's markets hurt manufacturers across the region.

Korean chaebols are alleged by some observers to be vastly overbuilding the capacity of their car factories in their eagerness to compete. The ability to manufacture cars has always been a fetish in developing countries but in Asia this has not meant merely assembling a few cars made elsewhere – in aggregate, Malaysia, Thailand and Indonesia will have the capacity to produce millions of their own cars annually by the turn of the century. China and India have allowed many major new automobile ventures but their people may not be able to afford to buy the vehicles once they are produced. Nor has there been much co-operation between countries in this field – each nation wants to be able to make its own vehicles *in toto* rather than specialising in particular areas of the industry. In justification of the drive to increase capacity, it is often pointed out that some Asian countries have virtually no cars at all – China, for instance, has fewer than 400,000 vehicles on the road and Vietnam has only 10,000 – but the question of whether mass car sales can be profitable remains unanswered.

In semi-conductors, Asian countries have specialised; South Korea is a world leader in producing memory chips, while silicon wafer production is concentrated in Taiwan and Singapore. Malaysia has had enormous success in developing assembly plants, serving major computer hardware corporations such as Motorola, Intel and Texas Instruments.

Prices of memory chips are plummeting as a glut hits the market, but there is no sign of a slackening of the pace. Malaysia and Singapore are building a large number of new silicon wafer plants, while major companies in Taiwan, such as Formosa Plastic, are eager to get into the industry – the island nation is constructing 12 silicon wafer factories at an estimated average cost of $1 billion each.

Employees in these factories are quick to learn, yet still earn remarkably low wages. The problem for the companies is how to keep wages low while attracting enough staff to continue growing; there are already signs that wage increases are outstripping productivity. Rapid growth has also created a lack of qualified technical managers – industry observers say that there aren't enough qualified chip engineers in the world to staff all the plants currently under construction.

In a free market, when there are too many companies making the same product some will go bankrupt and be absorbed by those that remain. State-backed manufacturers in Asia may be supported for too long when and if the predicted shake-out finally occurs. The winners are likely to be large manufacturers, such as Semiconductor Manufacturing in Taiwan and Chartered Semiconductor Manufacturing in Singapore.

Conclusion

The currency crisis may be a blessing in disguise. The IMF's stringent conditions are causing Korea, Thailand and Indonesia to begin to reform and restructure their economies and there is a growing recognition elsewhere in the region that the problems of success must be faced.

We can expect a greater emphasis in the future on education rather than construction. To shift to new markets and new industries, South East Asia as a whole needs better universities, better managers and, say the free marketeers, a more level playing field in business. Observers argue that industries such as private health care and the media could provide the answer to the problem of sustainable development – they're easier on the environment and would directly benefit the population.

Chapter 4

Easy Credit

Despite all the denials, it is now plain that had there not been such reckless lending in Asia, the crash would not have been as serious – it might not have happened at all.

Bankers are secretive. They also have a herd mentality. While all bankers pay lip-service to notions of careful lending and firm controls, banking crises happen with monotonous regularity across the world. As the economist Keynes famously pointed out, if you are a banker, it is relatively safe to be wrong when everyone else is wrong, since only a few heads will roll.

Asian commentators have rightly pointed out that their banking problems are not much different from previous scandals elsewhere, such as the US Savings and Loan debacle in the 1980s. Nevertheless, the way banking is supervised in the affected Asian countries clearly needs to be improved.

In this chapter we will look at how wanton lending has hurt the economies of Thailand, Korea and Indonesia. In each case, the easy money flowed through the system in a different way, reflecting the unique character of each country.

Thailand's property boom

In Thailand, people who wanted loans for property, cars, and other consumer durables went to the country's finance companies. These finance companies had found that it was easy to raise money by borrowing from abroad or by selling stocks and bonds to institutional investors – such as Korean banks.

In the early 1990s foreign lenders were falling over themselves to lend to Thai institutions and were not looking too closely at the financial fundamentals of the borrowers. Many banks in Asia, in particular, were so anxious to develop good relations with Thai banks that they were willing to lend simply to cement their relationships rather than to make profits.

This was good news for the finance companies in Thailand; they could borrow dollars cheaply and then lend baht to local consumers at high rates. From 14 to 20% was normal, not only for short-term consumer loans but also for property purchases. Property loans can only be sustained at such high rates if there is a property boom, but no-one seemed to care.

With plenty of cash, Thai finance companies and banks were looking for quick gains. They weren't interested in lending to productive sectors of the economy such as manufacturing – that meant hard work and a long wait before seeing a return.

In the early 1990s property was the way to make quick money in Thailand. Not only did the finance companies lend to property developers, but they themselves, like the high-flying Finance One, became involved in property speculation. Everyone was doing it – even the manufacturers began to channel their profits into property instead of ploughing it back into their businesses.

In Bangkok, you could see hundreds of construction cranes at work across the city. Skyscrapers were virtually popping up overnight like mushrooms. Nobody seemed to know who was going to occupy these buildings. Somehow, by magic, tenants and purchasers would appear.

By the end of 1995 there were no more occupants available. In Bangkok alone there were $20 billion worth of new buildings standing empty. A year later, they were still empty, and the speculators who had built them couldn't service their loans.

At the beginning of 1997 it has been estimated that there was up to $4 billion worth of 'non-performing' loans (banker's jargon for loans where the interest is not being paid). The Thai finance companies and banks could not afford to declare their real estate borrowers insolvent because their own financial standing would have been badly damaged. Instead, they covered up the problem and hoped it would go away.

Finance companies and banks did not press their borrowers too hard for interest payments, and disguised the truth by using creative accounting techniques. This worked for a while, but when Thailand's largest finance company, Finance One, and a big property company, Somprasong Land, failed to pay due debts to foreign lenders early in 1997, it became apparent to overseas observers that Thailand was in trouble.

The more sophisticated foreign lenders had no doubt been aware that Thai banks were not well run, but had relied on the Thai government's official and unofficial guarantees that banks would not be allowed to collapse.

By the spring of 1997, non-performing loans are thought to have been about a third of the country's GNP, a staggering figure, and it was clear that Thailand would not be able to cope with its insolvent banks on its own. Unlike Korea's collapse (see below) the problems had been caused by private borrowing.

Meanwhile, export growth had been slowing as India, China, Vietnam and Myanmar stepped up their own exports in competition. Thai wages were going up and their products were becoming too expensive by comparison.

Since the middle of 1996, the Bangkok Bank of Commerce (BBC) had been run by the government following revelations that it had lent $3 billion in non-performing loans. The beneficiaries included several government ministers and the late Rajan Pillai, a biscuit-maker and convicted swindler known as the 'Biscuit King,' who received over $100 million worth of baht.

By June 1997, all these problems coalesced; foreign investors pulled their money out if they could and the currency speculators pounced, sparking the crisis.

The Hanbo scandal in South Korea

In Korea, banks lent money hand-over-fist to the chaebol conglomerates while manufacturing sales declined. Minus some graft, most of the money went into capital investments whose true value is now in doubt.

The first big sign of trouble was in January 1997 when Hanbo Steel, a company in the Hanbo Group, defaulted on its loans. The scandal erupted when it was discovered that Hanbo, the country's 14th largest chaebol, which had grown immensely during the 1990s, had massive debts of around $US6 billion or 16 times its own capital.

Within days there were allegations of wrongdoing – how was it possible for any company to borrow so excessively? By February the then President Kim Young Sam gave a humiliating TV address apologising for the Hanbo collapse, saying:

> 'Whatever the reason ... all this is due to a lack of virtue on my part. I am responsible. With humility, I am willing to accept whatever reproach and criticism you make. As President, I express my sincere apology for the Hanbo case. The Hanbo case showed the shocking fact that corruption and the collusive link between politics and business remain deeply rooted in some parts of our society.'

Details began to emerge of bribery on a colossal scale, involving bankers, civil servants and members of the government. Hanbo's founder Chung Tae Soo had been handing out millions of dollars to anyone with influence in order to obtain the massive loans he needed to build the Tangjin steel mill, the fifth largest complex of its kind in the world.

At first there were moves to save Hanbo, but as ministers resigned and senior bankers were hauled before the courts it became plain that this was not a one-off problem; all the chaebols had been engaging in reckless expansion financed by extraordinarily high levels of borrowing.

Eventually the Hanbo group's chairman and his son were convicted of taking some US$400 million from the group to bribe government officials and bankers in a futile attempt to keep the group afloat.

Korean banks had traditionally been easily influenced by the government. They lent money according to the government's wishes, without regard for the soundness of the borrower. Bank directors' elections are influenced by the government, making them vulnerable to corrupt government officials.

Double-digit growth in Korea's plant capacity since 1995 had flooded markets with too many products, creating a growth in stock inventories, followed by price cuts. This in turn caused a drop in profits for Korean companies that left them helpless in the face of their crushing debts, commonly several times their equity.

The chaebols were having trouble paying the interest on their loans. Even in the tax year of 1996, when the economy grew at 7%, more than a third of the top 30 chaebols were losing money.

After the Hanbo problem was exposed, banks began taking a closer look at their loans and started calling in loans to the most indebted firms. That created a domino effect as more companies failed. The biggest blow came when Kia Motors, the country's eighth-largest chaebol, collapsed in July

1997 with debts bigger than Hanbo's. Kia's demise brought down one of the country's premier banks, the Korea First Bank.

As the currency crisis began in Thailand, it emerged that many Korean merchant banks had borrowed US dollars to buy high-risk bonds in Thai companies.

With such horrendous debts in industry and a disgraced banking sector, it was only a matter of time before Korea had to call in the IMF and agree to institute reforms.

At the time of writing, Korea is suffering. At the end of 1997 several of the world's largest banks, fearing a new wave of defaults, gave Korean borrowers a one-month reprieve on loan payments of up to $15 billion. 'If it got to a [debt repayment] moratorium in Korea, that likely would have spread to Indonesia and Thailand with a knock-on effect elsewhere,' said an American banker, 'The idea was to try and stop this at Korea.'

In 1997, over 15,000 companies went bankrupt and one million people lost their jobs. The Tangjin steel mill, which was the cause of Hanbo's overborrowing, has lost 80% of its workforce.

Indonesia

In the middle of 1996 there were massive anti-government demonstrations in Jakarta and foreign capital was expected to leave the country. The fact that it didn't was widely seen as evidence that foreign investors had confidence in the ability of the government to maintain both political and economic stability. Indonesian businesses went back to work. Interest rates within the country were as high as 18%, even for business loans, so companies went offshore to borrow at rates below 10%.

By 1997 private companies had borrowed more than $55 billion from foreign lenders, the equivalent of a quarter of the country's GNP.

Meanwhile, 'hot money' poured into Indonesia via the financial markets to buy short-term financial securities denominated in rupiah, taking advantage of the high local interest rates. This was not seen as unduly risky because of the Indonesian peg to the dollar, in effect a guarantee that the rupiah would not suddenly drop.

As in Thailand, banks were lending wildly to property developers, particularly for the construction of office buildings.

In all these respects, Indonesia resembled Thailand, but the country is at an earlier stage of economic development. With a vast population and wildly abundant natural resources, foreign lenders look upon the country with a more tolerant eye – they are more willing to accept irregularities in the way banks and businesses operate because of the archipelago's huge potential. Thailand, sadly, has industrialised itself so brutally that it has become less attractive to the long-term overseas investors.

Another important difference is that President Soeharto's government remains firmly in control and acted promptly to implement the IMF's requirements for reform. Even cherished enterprises such as banks and firms owned by members of the President's own family have been closed or had their operations restricted. The IMF has commended Indonesia for its co-operation. By contrast, Thailand fiercely resisted the IMF's demands for reform at first and it took a change of government for the state to face the reality of its situation.

The big question for Indonesia now is the political succession. President Soeharto is elderly – he's been in power since 1966 – and there is a new generation of young professionals, educated abroad, who are keen to see greater political and economic freedom. Doomsayers predict violence, even civil war, but *en masse* the population have so far been willing to accept the status quo in return for the increase in living standards they have enjoyed.

Chapter 5

The Lead Goose Falters –

Japan at the Crossroads

The economic development of the Asian countries has been likened to a flock of 'flying geese', all structured in similar ways and following the same basic strategies. The 'lead goose' is Japan, which established the path to modernisation which the rest have followed.

Now Japan is in trouble – not the same kind of trouble as South East Asia, but something far more profound.

Sponsored capitalism

It all started in the late nineteenth century when Japan, which had hitherto been an inward-looking feudal society, suddenly realised that it could not stand up to the modern weaponry of the West. The result was the Meiji Restoration, the reign of Emperor Mutsuhito from 1867 to 1912, during which Japan transformed itself by adopting a rapid process of Westernization, industrialisation and increased activity in foreign affairs. The Japanese willingness and ability to galvanise themselves overnight was regarded by the imperial powers as remarkable then, and today it is seen by many as the true origin of the Asian approach to capitalism.

The 'flying geese' do not practise the kind of capitalism that exists in the West, driven by the 'selfish' motives of private enterprise. Instead, they have what has been called 'sponsored capitalism', in which the government takes the lead in nurturing new industries and promoting economic development, sponsoring and chaperoning companies.

Prior to World War II, Japan's industry was run by 'zaibatsu', groups of large companies similar in nature to the Korean 'chaebol'.

During the US occupation after the war, Japan's zaibatsu were dissolved, but since the country's bureaucratic structure was preserved by the US Army, the same pre-war pattern of sponsored capitalism re-emerged to flourish in the post-war era.

This system has been extraordinarily successful over half a century, and Japan has become an economic superpower. Now its economy is stagnating; excessive government intervention and 'guidance' has resulted in a high-cost structure, lack of transparency and narrow-mindedness – a kind of economic arteriosclerosis.

For example, competitive principles do not function fully in many Japanese industries – totalling about 40% of the economy. As in other parts of Asia, Japanese society is very group-oriented. This has given rise to its system of lifetime employment, which has vastly increased the operating costs of Japanese corporations and is now recognised as a source of difficulty.

Japanese organisations generally operate on a consensus system that is alien to Western norms and while it has many benefits, it can sometimes result in a failure of leadership. This is what appears to be happening at present.

Almost everyone is agreed, both inside Japan and externally, that the country's economy is stagnating and has been doing so since the boom and bust of the late 1980s. There is little consensus on what should be done about it despite the unanimity on the apparent causes: the country has a weak financial sector, it is over-regulated, there is not enough competition, production has moved to South East Asia and so forth. All these suggest, in effect, that Japan, once touted as the world's most streamlined economy, has become inefficient and has excess production capacity.

Economists say that there could be an easy way to increase demand within the country. If the government were to increase public spending, or the Bank of Japan (the central bank) were to increase the amount of money in circulation, the public would have more money in its pocket to spend and banks would have more money to lend for private and commercial spending.

The Government and Bank of Japan appear to be reluctant to take this kind of action because of the trauma of the 1980s boom followed by the bust in the early 1990s. Readers may remember that ten years ago prices, particularly property prices, had become ludicrous in Japan, with tiny houses in Tokyo going for millions of dollars, the Imperial Palace becoming technically worth more than the whole of California and single golf club memberships going for $1 million. The authorities apparently believe that a loosening of the money supply would simply result in another unhealthy bubble.

Instead, Japan talks of structural reform. Whatever the merits of such reforms, they are unlikely to cure the stagnation fast. The consensus-building process is slow and while there is agreement on broad principles, the details of the reform packages and their implementation are not known or have not yet been decided. The only certainty is that any reforms will be undertaken in a way that minimises unemployment.

In October 1996 Japan's Liberal Democratic Party won power in a landslide election. The new Prime Minister, Ryutaro Hashimoto, immediately committed himself to a programme of six fundamental reforms aimed at:

1   administrative reform
2   fiscal reform
3   structural transformation of the economy

4   reform of the financial system
5   reform of the social security system
6   educational reform.

In addition, Hashimoto reaffirmed Japan's commitment to its politico-economic alliance with the USA, saying:

> 'The continued engagement of the United States in the Asia-Pacific region is desirable for the entire region, both in security and socioeconomic spheres. Together with President Bill Clinton, beginning his second term in office today, I intend to make my utmost efforts to further strengthen the good Japan–U.S. relationship as the foundation of Japan's foreign policy. In particular, recognising that the Japan–U.S. Security Arrangements are not only essential for the peace and security of Japan but are also extremely important for the overall Asia-Pacific region, I intend to work to further increase their credibility through such measures as a review of the Guidelines for Japan–US Defense Cooperation. In keeping with the basic idea of an exclusively defense-oriented policy under the Constitution and of never becoming a military power which might pose a threat to other countries, the Government is determined to firmly uphold civilian control and adhere to the three non-nuclear principles. In line with the New National Defense Program Outline and the New Mid-Term Defense Program, Japan seeks to streamline its defense capability and to make it more effective and compact, while enhancing its functions and making qualitative improvements. Likewise, for confidence-building in the realm of security in the Asia-Pacific region, we will promote security dialogue, beginning with the ASEAN Regional Forum, as well as various defense exchanges.'

The US also frequently affirms that Japan is its main partner in Asia. Together they make up two of the world's three powerful economic blocs, the other being Western Europe. The US supports Japan's goal of obtaining a permanent seat on the United Nations Security Council. The two governments work closely together to address global issues, not only those in Asia, such as the environment, technology development, and health.

Political developments had been regarded with some scepticism in the US, where the media had reported that the door to reform and transformation was closed when the LDP increased its parliamentary representation in the recent election and had suggested that Hashimoto would not implement any real reforms. Perhaps this arises from Western bemusement at the consensual process that is undoubtedly going on. In Japan, at any rate, the talk of reform is being taken seriously, but always in the context of close co-operation between the government and business in the first place, and close co-operation between management and the workforce in the second.

Japan's foreign aid

It is not generally appreciated in the West just how active Japan has been in donating aid abroad. By using aid, Japan can influence the way Asia develops without having to open its own markets to foreign competition, an action that it has been notoriously reluctant to take.

Since 1991, Japan has given away more money than any other nation. In 1970 Japan was giving Asia 98% of its aid budget, but by the 1990s this figure has dropped to a little over 50%.

In pursuit of its aim to keep the 'flying geese' in formation, Japan has been using its aid program in Asia to further a plan of development for the whole region.

Prior to the currency crisis, Japan's main focus had been on assisting the ex-communist countries, such as Vietnam, to shift to market economies, not only by advising its governments on how to devise their series of five-year plans but also to give Japanese-style training along 'zaibatsu' lines.

From 1985 onwards Japan's industries had begun moving their factories to cheaper Asian countries in order to keep their share of world markets and their products competitive despite the strong yen.

A 'New Asian Industries Development Plan' was devised, which called for extremely close co-operation between Asian countries along the lines of Japan's own internal planning methods, which would give the developing countries what they strongly desired – namely the ability to export higher value-added goods – while helping Japanese companies to establish their production facilities abroad.

Thus, Thailand was to concentrate on products such as textiles, plastic goods and toys, Malaysia on personal computers, office equipment and rubber goods, Indonesia on electrical machinery, ceramics and rubber goods, the Philippines on computer software and furniture, and so on. Experts were to be sent from Japan to all these countries, industrial parks were planned and cheap loans were made available to build the necessary infrastructure and finance the businesses. Ultimately, Japan was to allow some of these products into its own internal markets.

These schemes were extraordinarily detailed and elaborate, amounting to a masterpiece of central planning for virtually the whole of Asia – including countries such as India and Pakistan.

The developing countries have not been wholly enthusiastic about this initiative -there was a sense of gentle coercion, and some feared that they might be frozen out of regional trade if they did not co-operate entirely. By 1987 the scheme had foundered, apparently because of internal rivalries in the Japanese civil service. Aid policy seems to have become less all-encompassing, but the fact remains that there are elements in Japan who see the notion of the country's 'lead goose' status as more than just a description of a natural phase in the economic evolution of Asia.

Yamaichi

One of the central areas of reform in Japan is to be the finance sector, which never properly recovered from the chaos of the early 1990s crash.

In the autumn of 1997, a series of bankruptcies among financial institutions sent panic around Asia's stock markets – could it be that Japan, too, had caught the 'Asian contagion'?

Prime Minister Hashimoto was quick to point out that Japan's difficulties were utterly different from the currency problems in South East Asia, affirming that his country, as the world's second-largest economy, could solve its financial problems internally and would have no need of bail-outs.

Nevertheless, the sight of the collapse of the century-old Yamaichi Securities Co. Ltd, Japan's fourth largest stockbroker, was daunting. No Japanese firm of its size had ever collapsed before, and the dramatic photographs of the company's president, Shohei Nozawa, weeping as he apologised at a press conference for the company's failure, were printed everywhere.

'I express deep regret', he said, 'and I really feel sorry for our employees. I sincerely hope you will give them support to find new jobs.'

The mood within the firm can perhaps be gauged by the death of a 38-year-old accounting section chief who died at home after working non-stop without leaving for 14 days during the collapse – a phenomenon known in Japan as 'karoshi,' or death from overwork. On the same day, an employee of a company affiliated with Yamaichi jumped to his death from a building in the financial district of Osaka.

At first it appeared that Yamaichi had been crushed by the 80% drop in its share price and a massive debt hangover of some 3 trillion yen ($23.6 billion) from the 1980s bubble, but soon stories began to emerge of illegal payoffs to corporate racketeers and 'off-balance sheet' (i.e. concealed) liabilities.

While these practices are believed to be widespread in Japan, there was general outrage at reports that the off-balance sheet liabilities exceeded 200 billion yen ($1.58 billion) and that they had arisen from illegal trading practices in which brokers temporarily shift investment losses from one client to another in order to prevent a favoured customer from having to report losses. These debts were hidden in dummy companies in the British dependency of the Cayman Islands.

Among the company's favoured clients were prominent politicians. Yamaichi had agreed to transactions where a client sold shares and bonds at a loss and bought them back at higher-than-market prices – an activity known as 'tobashi'. The firm hoped to recover its losses in the future on profitable transactions.

In the past, the principle of mutual co-operation had meant that firms in this kind of trouble would be supported by the central bank and any scandal could be played down. Now the government was no longer willing to do so, and the country's newspapers bellowed that Japan's financial system was in urgent need of reform, deregulation, closer supervision and transparency.

The spate of institutional bankruptcies is expected to continue as more hidden debts come to light.

Japan's financial crisis

The financial system is in a state of uproar, but it is not a terminal disease. Company treasurers are having difficulties in rolling over debt as banks have suddenly tightened their lending policies.

Liquidity problems are expected to cause unemployment as weaker companies go under.

Despite popular fears of government bail-outs, the ruling LDP has finally come up with a 30 trillion yen package to support the troubled banks. The public mood is angry – there is evidently a feeling that individual bankers should receive no protection and should be made personally bankrupt.

The media are baying for blood, pointing out that after the Savings and Loans scandal in the USA, some 1600 S & L managers were sent to prison. This comparison may be irrelevant, but it is surely evidence that Japan really does want its reforms.

Chapter 6

The Great Game

Now that the initial alarm is over, the 1997 crisis is becoming more intelligible. It began, essentially, with incompetent banking. All countries have state guarantees for their banking system, but it is normal for these guarantees to have strict conditions – the shareholders of private banks must risk their own capital, central banks must supervise their operations strictly, banks must lend prudently with the intention of getting their money back and so on.

In the affected countries, privileged individuals were allowed access to vast sums of money, either as bankers or as business borrowers, so freely that it was plain to the more astute among them that they themselves would not have to pay the money back – the government would do it for them. As they ploughed fortunes into speculative investments and over-ambitious business projects, naïve foreign investors fell over themselves to provide even more money for the region, mesmerised by the spectacle of rapid growth. Foolish loans made stock markets and property prices overvalued, which in turn made the accounts of banks and business borrowers look better than they really were.

Thus Asia's 'real' growth became overlaid by a speculative bubble which, in hindsight, had to burst sometime.

It is interesting to see that East Asia falls into three different groups with regard to the crisis:

- Japan and Korea, who have recognised for some years that their economic structures are in need of reform, in particular the way in which their industries are financed.
- South East Asia, which had been growing at high speed, but was borrowing enormous amounts of foreign money and had an unsound banking sector.
- China and the sophisticated city states of Hong Kong and Singapore, who have, so far, fought off the crisis and continued to enjoy healthy growth, strong trade surpluses and large reserves of foreign exchange.

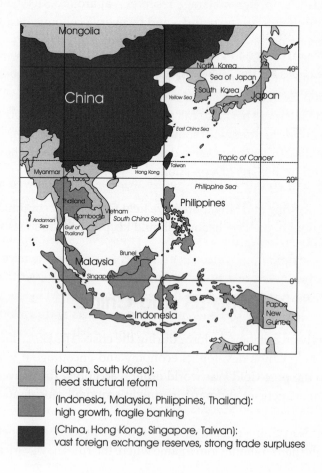

(Japan, South Korea):
need structural reform

(Indonesia, Malaysia, Philippines, Thailand):
high growth, fragile banking

(China, Hong Kong, Singapore, Taiwan):
vast foreign exchange reserves, strong trade surpluses

Taiwan, which also has a strong economy, chose not to defend its currency strongly when the crisis hit, but allowed it to devalue. This increased the pressure on Hong Kong, which suffered a big drop in its stock market. Observers speculate on Taiwan's motives. It did have the money to defend itself had it wished to do so and there is talk that it may have sought to embarrass China by forcing Hong Kong to abandon its exchange rate peg, thus discrediting the smooth transition of the island back to Chinese control.

Taiwan has vast foreign exchange reserves – at around $100 billion, they are the third largest in the world – and by every economic measure it remained strong despite the chaos in the region.

Thus another interpretation of its actions is that this was a 'competitive devaluation' designed to make its exports more attractive. Voices in Hong Kong and Singapore began to call for the abandonment of their currency pegs. This was regarded with some horror by Western observers who recalled the disastrous competitive devaluations of the 1930s which were a major factor in the Great Depression.

So far, Hong Kong and Singapore have held firm. If they continue to do so for long enough, the IMF bailouts should keep the situation stable.

The US and China

China has been a stabilising force during the crisis. The USA's main objective is to help China develop its economy and encourage it to integrate itself into the post-Cold War world order – accepting the conventions of international agencies and participating in economic globalisation.

Some voices in China remain suspicious of the process, and openly wonder why the nation should join a game where the rules have very evidently been written by the wealthy capitalist nations. There are fears that if China opens its doors too widely, it will be dominated by the very powers that it had regarded as enemies for 50 years.

There are signs that the US is willing to give China the opportunity to, as it were, change the rules of the global game to some extent. While the West aims for the advancement of human rights, free trade and sustainable growth, China is more interested in emphasising such matters as non-interference in the internal affairs of nation states by agencies like the UN. For every concession it makes to capitalism, it tends to want something in return, an attitude that sometimes confuses Americans, who often regard such concessions as obligatory. The ideological gap between the two superpowers remains profound.

Dean LeBaron, founder of Batterymarch Financial Management in the US and a respected emerging market investor, writes that:

> 'Linking human rights and business always struck me as a bad idea. Bad for business and bad for the human rights activists, whose arrests tend to increase when the U.S. brings pressure to bear; if not immediately, then soon after. For any number of reasons the Chinese Communist Party is unlikely to give way; both because of traditional fear of losing face and the real need of the Party to demonstrate power when it no longer has the regalia of ideology to lend it credibility and legitimacy. Both ends, greater democracy and greater trade, are worthy; the error is linking them.

> 'There are those who believe that democracy will come to China naturally, by the creation of a middle class and through the independence of thought that seems to follow electronic communication − computer chips are the apple seeds of free thought. To some degree, I share that belief. I indicated as much when I addressed SITICO, saying it was

TV, not the demolition crews, that brought down the Berlin Wall. But Germany, and even the Soviet Union, are one thing. China is quite another. The Germans discovered painful problems that no one had foreseen on the nights of reunification amid all the champagne and euphoria. Even the fate of the Soviet Union is, for China, an example to be avoided.'

Climbing Falling Walls by Dean LeBaron is available in its entirety at his Web site: http://www.deanlebaron.com

Avoiding a world recession

If the crisis is not resolved and Hong Kong and Singapore have to devalue their currencies drastically, the 'contagion' is likely to spread across the world, say economists, first to Brazil and other emerging markets, ultimately stifling global trade in general. The USA's massive trade deficit would increase, slowing the country's growth, and providing fuel for the protectionists who would like to raise barriers against Asia's exports. A protectionist US – probably followed by a protectionist Europe – would leave troubled countries on their own with no markets to sell to, raising the bogey of a worldwide recession.

Conversely, if currency markets turned on the US dollar, inflation and interest rates would rise dramatically in the Western nations and their stock markets could collapse – an event which is in any case long overdue, in the opinion of actuaries.

The West wants economic and currency stability in Asia; so does Asia. By the end of 1998 it should be clear whether this has been achieved.

Conclusion

The IMF is fast becoming a kind of global bankruptcy court, and its member countries need to agree on the powers it should have for its role of helping to prevent financial crises before they occur. The Asia Pacific Monetary Fund (APEC) may be given authority over any 'Asian monetary fund' that is created by the region. Globalisation is forcing more and more international co-operation. The nations of the world are more interdependent than ever. Meanwhile an argument is raging over whether there should be more bail-out money available – increasing the risk of 'moral hazard', where spendthrift countries might feel an incentive to continue with profligate policies, knowing that they would be helped if they ran into financial trouble – or whether the system of *ad hoc* loans should continue, which is risky because they might, one day, simply not materialise.

Index

FT Profile

Part of this book was written using FT Profile.

FT Profile is an easy-to-use database containing a vast amount of business and professional information provided by some 5000 sources, and is constantly updated. To access it, all you need is a PC and a telephone line. Here is a brief selection of some of the information available:

- Company profiles, reports and accounts for major companies across the world.
- More than 100,000 broker research reports on thousands of companies worldwide, provided by Investext and ICC.
- Massive international news coverage from many sources, including the *Financial Times*, the *Washington Post*, the *American Banker* and *Agence France-Presse*.
- Business news from providers such as *Forbes*, *Money Management*, *Asia Week*, *The Economist* and *Business Week*. Country Reports from the Economist Intelligence Unit.
- Possibly the most comprehensive database for detailed business information on Asia, via 'Asia Intelligence Wire'.
- Detailed market research reports on a wide range of industries, including electronics, food, healthcare, household products, building engineering and chemicals across the world.

Dedicated international investors will also be able to use the database to monitor political and regulatory changes affecting plans.

Commercial rates for using FT Profile are on a 'pay as you go' basis, plus a one-off registration charge, currently £250. Costs depend on the time you spend on the system, (there is a connection charge of 40p a minute) and which sources you access (news files cost 4p per line, while some market research costs 40p per line). Internet users, however, will be pleasantly surprised at the rapidity with which large amounts of data can be downloaded onto their PC for subsequent perusal. FT Profile is provided by Financial Times Electronic Publishing.

CAPSTONE

If you enjoyed ASIA MELTDOWN you will be interested in some of our other titles. Please order through your local bookseller or in case of difficulty via Capstone (see details overleaf):

Mastering the Infinite Game: How Asian Values are Transforming Business Practices
Charles Hampden-Turner
£18.99
1 900961 08 3
Examines the cultural dynamics of Asian economies that are generating wealth at bewildering speed.

Blur: the speed of change in the connected economy
Stan Davis and Christopher Meyer
£16.99
1 900961 71 7
'*Blur* is fast, smart and useful. A decoder ring that anybody can use to make sense of the turbulence in the world of work today.'
Alan Webber, Founding Editor, *Fast Company* magazine

Break Up: When large companies are worth more dead than alive
David Sadtler, Andrew Campbell and Richard Koch
£7.99
1 900961 39 3
Analyses the growing phenomenon of demergers and shows why it is a compelling and even necessary option for shareholders and managers alike.

The Emperor's Nightingale
Robert A.G. Monks
£18.99
1 900961 29 6
'A compelling vision of the corporation of the future by a champion of corporate accountability.'
George Soros

Synergy: Why links between business units often fail and how to make them work
Andrew Campbell and Michael Goold
£18.99
1 900961 57 1
'*Synergy* is a thoughtful, thorough approach to an opportunity that has long eluded many corporations. The authors use their considerable experience to create practical tools for managers at both corporate centers and business units, showing how the whole can truly become more valuable than the sum of the parts.'
Rosabeth Moss Kanter, Harvard Business School, author of *Rosabeth Moss Kanter on the Frontiers of Management*

Inside the Tornado: Marketing strategies from Silicon Valley's cutting edge
Geoffrey A. Moore
£9.99
1900961 58 X
'The Chasm is where many high-tech fortunes have been lost ... the Tornado is where many have been made.'
Steve Jobs, founder and CEO, NeXT Computer Inc

Salmon Day: The end of the beginning for global business
Douglas Lamont
£18.99
1 900961 19 9
Salmon Day is the experience of spending entire day swimming upstream only to get screwed in the end. Although computer jargon, it is a perfect metaphor for global business where massive initiatives frequently flounder. *Salmon Day* is a radical redrawing of the global business map for executives who are already looking to the future.

Capstone Publishing
Oxford Centre for Innovation
Mill Street
Oxford OX1 0JX
Tel: +44 1865 798623
Fax: +44 1865 240941
E-mail: capstone_publishing@msn.com
http://www.capstone.co.uk